Best Wishes Barlee

LuMarie

10-1-06

# JUSTICE FOR LORINDA

## And other lives destroyed

by

LinMarie Garsee

Bloomington, IN  Milton Keynes, UK

author HOUSE™

AuthorHouse™
1663 Liberty Drive, Suite 200
Bloomington, IN 47403
www.authorhouse.com
Phone: 1-800-839-8640

AuthorHouse™ UK Ltd.
500 Avebury Boulevard
Central Milton Keynes, MK9 2BE
www.authorhouse.co.uk
Phone: 08001974150

First published by AuthorHouse 7/10/2006

ISBN: 1-4259-4472-8 (sc)

Printed in the United States of America
Bloomington, Indiana

This book is printed on acid-free paper.

This book is dedicated to all,
Both living or deceased
Who have lived the life or are living the life
Of a battered victim.

I pray you will find your way out of
The circumstances without harm
And that along the way
You will find peace….

LinMarie

# ACKNOWLEDGMENTS

I can never begin to thank those who have encouraged me or who have read and reread the manuscript or just listened to me talk about it.

Jesse Gomez, Reggie Johnson & Charlie Ryan for believing in me and helping with research & education

Fred Power for always being a friend

Bettina & Tim Elliott for the background information & running errands for me in the Valley

Harlingen Police Department (Captain Ramon Vela & Rebecca Morales) & Cameron County Texas District Clerk's office for their responses to my requests

Rachael Coe for the medical information and always saying "Go for it, you can do it!"

Sandi Hudson, for reading and rereading the manuscript when she had other things on her plate

The past and present acquaintances (including ex-roommates of Tony's who are still incarcerated - you know who you are) of Tony's who talked to me willingly and provided a wealth of information on both Tony and Lorinda

And, last, but not least, my friend Miechael Eaves who let me bounce things off of her and was friend enough to tell me when I was wrong

And more than anything, I thank God that I was given the wisdom to know when to hold 'em and when to fold 'em; and, for the protection He has given me throughout both of my books that I not only wrote, but lived.

To Patrick and Travis, you will always be my Two Hearts

To Jesse for putting up with me when I needed to bounce questions or ideas off of you and giving me the time to write.

And, to the girlfriends for standing by me in the thick of it all: Miechael Eaves, Margaret Ann Smith, Pat Williams, Donna Garcia, Sandi Hudson, Jackie Martin, Martha Sundermeyer, Rachael Coe, Tammy Grimes, Karon McGaha, Mildred Holman, Bettina Elliott and Willie Mae Lewis. Your prayers and faith have kept me going!

To Ryan for keeping the computer updated and in tip top shape .

To Reggie for always being a phone call away.

To the Managements of Chamberlain Cemetery & Turcotte Funeral Home in Kingsville, Texas.

To the special man who edited this for me -

This is for all of you. Many thanks.

LinMarie

When I first wrote to Jose Antonio "Tony" Gonzalez, Jr., he was housed at the Wynne Unit Farm, a division of the Texas Department of Criminal Justice Institutional Division located in Huntsville, Texas. I was working for an attorney who prepared parole packets. A parole packet is information compiled about the inmate which could show the Board of Pardons and Parole why an inmate is a good candidate for parole. Such packets would include letters from family and friends in support of the inmate being released to come home, the inmate's disciplinary records, an explanation of the crime, the inmate's goals, how the inmate plans to integrate back into society, as well as any classes, schools, or industrial work the inmate may have done while he or she was incarcerated. Mr. Gonzalez (sometimes spells his name Gonzales) had asked that I come to discuss his prospective parole. I was also told that "Tony", as he preferred to be called, was an excellent silver smith.

Tony, in 2001, right off the bat, told me that he had survived prison on his own. Tony was, by all of his accounts, a self made man. Tony said his parents had never given him a dime during his entire incarceration. Tony went on to say that he started out in the craft shop working for other inmates until he saved enough money to get involved in the craft shop on his own. Tony said he had gotten contracts for crafts from guards and prison officials to do work for others outside of the prison. While Tony was incarcerated I

1

purchased several silver items made, which I thought were made by him. Now, I do not know for certain that it was Tony who made them and I know for certain that Tony's family did support him during his incarceration.

To tell his story, I must go back in time to where it all began.

Harlingen, Texas, lies on the southern part of the Texas Gulf Coast about 30 miles north of the Mexico border. In Texas, it is part of what is known as The Rio Grande Valley. It boasts of its delicious citrus orchards, lush vegetation, manicured yards, year round golf courses that can be played on pretty much year round, an abundance of winter Texans who drive from the north down south in the winter, the dog races, and an AAA baseball team. The weather exceeds 100 degrees in the summer time. Museums are abundant including the Butterfly Museum, The Harlingen Marine Military Academy and the Confederate Air Force Museum. Just to the south of Harlingen is the Rio Grande River and south of that is Mexico.

The name Rio Grande is sort of a metaphor, considering that in Spanish it means Big River - but, yet, the river is not so big, not so deep - however, a definite divider between the United States and Mexico.

Jose' Antonio Gonzalez, Jr. was born September 11, 1961 in Mercedes, Texas. He was the older of what would be four children either born to or adopted by his parents, Tony, Sr. and Catalina Gonzalez.

Tony went to school at Bowie Elementary, Coakley Middle School, and later Harlingen High School, all located in Harlingen, Texas.

A friend of his, Bettina Anzaldua, described her relationship with Tony during their youth by stating, *"Tony and I met in Mrs. Gonzales' [a teacher and no relation to Tony] Spanish class at Coakley Middle School in Harlingen. I was in 9th grade and 14 years old, Tony was in 8th and was 16. I had not lived in Harlingen very long and I didn't have*

2

*a lot of close friends. Having attended three schools my 8th grade year in three different cities, I wasn't having "the best years of my life" as so many forgetful adults seem to call them."*

*"I was a bit shocked to meet someone two years older than me, but a year behind me in school. Tony seemed bright, articulate, didn't come across as "a loser" or "a scum bag" as many of our peers did. He had such a pleasant smile. We would see each other walking home from school so we began what was to be one of my few close friendships thru out my "school life."*

*"Tony lived about a block away from my house on Lincoln. Even as I went on to high school and he was still at middle school, we maintained our friendship & it grew to a deep closeness I didn't have with anyone else at the time. Tony knew things about me no one else knew, but I trusted him completely and to my knowledge, he never betrayed that trust."*

*"A true friend knows your secrets but loves you anyway. I felt like this was the relationship Tony and I shared. We never had any sort of romantic involvement with each other. If he had anything like that in mind, at any time, he never let on. We actually began referring to each other as brother and sister somewhere along the line. There were many who believed we were siblings. We said we had different fathers, that was why we had different last names. Well, it wasn't a lie, we did have different fathers."*

Tony had his male buddies during high school as well. One of them was Noe Garza. Noe stated that "Growing up we were in the road. We graduated from Boone's Farm to Southern Comfort. Tony was the shorter of all of us, but he always had a woman. He was a prankster too."

Noe also stated, "Tony never wanted for a date. But he was the party animal. And he could or tried to control people all the time, even when we were kids."

After High School Tony started working for Valley Baptist Hospital. He and Lorinda Rocha had been dating since High School.

Lorinda, or Lori as she preferred to be called, was just younger than Tony. She was, according to her friends, "the best friend anyone could ever have. She was beautiful."

There is little known of Lorinda Rocha's life. When I contacted her parents regarding this book, no one responded. However, they did tell a friend of Lorinda's that they saw no future in dredging up old, hurtful memories of the incident. It wasn't an "incident" - it was murder.

Clarissa described Lorinda as "a gorgeous, flirty type girl with an outgoing personality. Lori would walk into a room and was like a magnet - everyone would be attracted to her. She was in drama. [Though research at Harlingen High School did not show Lori in drama, nor any extracurricular activities.] She always wore her hair short. She was real petite - just really cute. And, she was a friend to the end - you could tell Lori anything and it would never leave her. She was an All-American girl."

Lorinda graduated from Harlingen High School a year after Tony did, in 1982. She was enrolled at Pan American University at the time of her death.

Tony was deceitful even in his youth. A friend of Lorinda's stated, "Tony had a way of making people who weren't as intelligent as he, believe he was something he wasn't. He had Lori believing he was a doctor."

It was this deceit that allows this story to continue.

On November, 18, 1983, Lorinda Rocha checked in at the Motel 6 located in Harlingen, Texas. The following morning, she was found dead.

Maria Pena, a maid working at the Motel 6 would find the charred body of Lorinda Rocha on November 19th, 1983.

*Clarrisa stated, "Tony had a way of making people who weren't as intelligent as he believe he was something he wasn't. He had Lori believing that he was a doctor because he was 22 and worked at a hospital. That's why she was letting him perform the abortion. He was just real convincing and Lori was just real gullible. Tony was a master manipulator."

*Clarissa and Lori's sister, Renee, knew that Lori was pregnant and that Tony was going to perform an abortion. Renee was only in the 9th grade at Coakley Junior High School and Clarissa was only 15 years old at the time. Having not told any adult that Lori was pregnant, much less about having an abortion, Clarrisa, to this day, has deep regrets that she might have been able to have saved her friend.

Lori had broken up with Tony just prior to the fire. When Lori found out that she was pregnant by Tony, she would tell Renee, "the reason she started to be with him again  was for only using him for the abortion. Lorinda said that Tony was going to perform the abortion and give her some type of an injection."

The death of Lori was not an accident. It was a planned and calculated act that even in 2004 Tony blames Lorinda for. Tony has made the statement, referring to Lori, "The bitch deserved to die because she was ruining my life with having that baby."

In talking to several of Lorinda's friends it was common knowledge that Lorinda was pregnant and the father of the child was Jose Antonio "Tony" Gonzalez, Jr. who was the ex-boyfriend of Lorinda.

Lorinda told Benito Valdez, Jr. the morning that she checked into the hotel room that evening, on November 18, 1983, that Tony Gonzalez was going to perform the abortion that night and she was scared Tony would hurt her.

Lorinda also told [Clarissa] that Tony had tried once before to help her abort the baby and he used chloroform to put her under, but it didn't work.

On November 17, 1983, Clarissa had dinner at Lorinda's house and Lorinda told Clarissa "tomorrow is the day." When Clarissa asked Lorinda what she meant, Lorinda said, "Tony is going to perform the abortion tomorrow night", which would have been November 18, 1983.

"I know this is personal, but after they would have sex, he was so rough with her that she would bleed for days. He is a sadistic pervert. I do know that Tony had to have control of everything. What she did, where she went. He was extremely domineering. Lori was really afraid of her dad and what he would do if he found out that she was pregnant." stated Clarissa.

*Clarissa is a tell it like it is person. She is an outspoken, funny, educated woman who knows what she wants from life; and, she is an achiever. She is a transplanted Valleyite, originally from Tennessee. It is obvious in speaking with her, that this tragedy, occurring in her younger years, has immensely affected her - even in her adult life.

It was Clarissa's request that her name be kept confidential, as she feared retribution from Tony - even today.

"On November 19, 1983 at 11:03 a.m., the Harlingen Police Department received a call from Tom Trewin, manager of Motel 6 located at 224 South U.S. Expressway 77, Harlingen, Texas. Mr. Trewin reported that two of his cleaning ladies found a badly burned body of an individual in Room #51 at Motel 6," Captain Doster of the Harlingen Police Department's report would read.

Captain Doster's report went on to say, "A check with Oscar Gutierrez who is a desk clerk at Motel 6 revealed [that] a young lady who identified herself as Lorinda Rocha rented Room #51 at approximately

9:00 p.m., November 18, 1983. Mr. Gutierrez stated the young lady showed him a Texas Driver's License for identification and she rented the room for two persons. However, she was alone when she rented the room."

"Detective Sergeant Crispin C. Trevino and Detective Robert Rapp went to 2013 Adrian Street and contacted the parents of Lorinda Rocha. The parents advised the two detectives that Lorinda had left the house between 8:00 and 8:30 p.m. on the 18th of November, 1983 and they had not heard or seen Lorinda since. The parents were advise of what was found [in Room 51] at Motel 6."

Of course, the next of kin, husband or boyfriend are the first suspects and the first to be contacted. Tony was a suspect from day one.

"On December 13, 1983, Jose Antonio Gonzalez, Jr. was asked if he would take a polygraph and he said he would. Jose Antonio Gonzalez, Jr. was taken to the Texas Department of Public Safety in McAllen, Texas and administered a polygraph examination by S. A. Robles. The test did indicate deception at questions pertaining to knowledge of and/or participation in this offense [Lorinda's death]. On December 27, 1983, Jose Antonio Gonzalez, Jr. was called by Captain John Doster and he [Tony] was asked if he would come in to the Harlingen Police Department so he could be interviewed about the Rocha case. He said he would come in and he showed up at the police station at about 10:30 a.m. During the interview, Jose Antonio Gonzalez, Jr. admitted giving Lorinda chloroform and trying to abort the baby. After something went wrong and Tony thought Lorinda was dead, he caused [set] a fire to be started, burning the bed and the body of Lorinda Rocha."

In a statement given to police, Lourdes Valenzuela, a co-worker, at the time of the fire and dated December 29, 1983, Lourdes stated, "On November 18, 1983, while on duty at the hospital, Tony Gonzalez, who is also a hospital employee who works at the lab as a collector, came by the lab at approximately 4 PM to pick up a beeper as he was on call. After signing out with the beeper, Tony advised Mario Gonzales, another hospital employee, and I that if he went to Brownsville, he would call in and advise us and he left. At approximately 11 PM as I was getting ready to get off-duty, Tony Gonzales came into the lab thru the rear door. Tony walked right past me, walking as if he was in a hurry. I was extremely surprise[d], as Tony would usually stop and visit for awhile. Mario Gonzales asked Tony as he passed by if he was going to work. Tony did not answer Mario, and Tony continued walking into the lab. I would further like to state that when Tony first came in he was dressed very neatly. I believe that he was wearing a beige sport shirt and blue jeans and when he returned his shirt was out and disarranged and it appeared to me that he had just gotten up from sleeping."

Mario Gonzales, another co-worker would state in his report to the police, that Tony "also appeared to be pre-occupied about something. He just was not acting the same." regarding his memory of the visit to the lab on November 18th.

According to police reports that were filed at the time of the fire, Officer Jesus Venegas wrote: "November 19, 1983, I was dispatched, along with other officers to Room Number 51 in the Motel 6 which is located in Harlingen, Texas. The purpose of my investigation was to assist fellow officers with the discovery of a burned body in that particular room."

"Upon our arrival, Officer Silva and I entered the motel room and, being careful not to disturb the scene, began to check the area for possible weapons or anything which might have given us an idea as to what had actually occurred. After taking an initial look and not finding anything such as a weapon or anything else which might indicate a cause of death, Officer Leo Silva then began to take pictures of the scene."

"Looking at where the body laid, I saw that it appeared that the fire appeared to have been more intense on the northwest corner of the bed. The bed was not totally burned. I also saw that the body that lay on the bed was charred beyond recognition. When the morticians removed the bed covers off the body, I saw that the heaviest burning occurred to the upper part of the body above the abdomen. Also, with the removal of the bed covers, I saw that the female had bled from her vaginal area, but at that time I attributed it to the intense heat of the room during the fire."

"After leaving the scene, I discovered that the female inside the motel room was Lorinda Rocha. I had known her to have been the girlfriend of Antonio Gonzales. I then spoke with Mr. Gonzales later in the day, and he claimed that he had no knowledge as to what had become of her."

One police report reads, "At the scene investigators found the body of a young female laying in bed on her back. The covers were neatly tucked in next to her body. The top part of her body was burned and the top part of the bed was also burned... Justice of the Peace Pinky Dirks was called to the scene and pronounced the victim dead and he ordered an autopsy performed. Identification found in a purse at the scene showed the purse belonged to Lorinda Rocha...The autopsy revealed that the young lady found in Room #51 was pregnant."

Dr. Lawrence J. Dahm, Pathologist wrote his pathologic diagnoses as:

1. Thermal burns over most of the body:

   A. Third and 4th degree burns of head, anterior chest, arms, hands and upper abdomen.

   B. Second-degree burns of lower abdomen and anterior thighs

   C. Evidence of hot gas and soot inhalation.

2. Chloroform intoxication.

3. Pregnancy, late first trimester.

Summary: This young pregnant woman died of burns caused by a fire in her bed, while she lay in the bed. She was under the influence of chloroform, as confirmed by toxicologic analysis of her blood. The fire is stated to have been deliberately set, in the opinion of consultant arson investigators. This young woman was breathing at the time the fire began, as there was soot inhaled into the trachea, larynx and bronchi. In our opinion, the cause of death is thermal burning by fire; the manner of death is homicide."

"No evidence of genital tract trauma or attempted criminal abortion was found."

"Drug and alcohol tests on the blood, as well as carbon monoxide determinations are all negative. Special procedures to look for volatile compounds in the blood reveal 30 mg/liter of chloroform."

"There is a corpus luteum of pregnancy in the right ovary."

"Vaginal smears reveal only vaginal and cervical mucosal squamous cells. No red blood cells or sperm are identified. Most of the tissue show severe autolytic changes."

"Carbonaceous particles are found in the lumens of the mainstem bronchi. They are too large and too plentiful to be accounted for by cigarette smoke inhalation."

Chloroform is a heavy colorless liquid with a characteristic odor and sweet taste. It is non-inflammable. It is very irritating when applied to the mucous membranes or to the skin. As an anesthetic, it is very rapid in action; a few drops on a mask will produce unconsciousness. The margin of safety is small; it is a dangerous drug to use, and its use should be limited to those who have had extensive training and experience in this field. Due to its quick action, it has at times been employed to commit a murder. This is usually done by pouring a considerable quantity on a cloth and holding it over the victim's face. Under such conditions, the gas is so concentrated that the breath is shut off and death from asphyxiation takes place rapidly.

Some persons are very susceptible to poisoning from chloroform. This produces jaundice and death a few hours after its administration. An autopsy, will reveal a fatty degeneration of the liver; sometimes the degeneration will also be found in the kidneys and heart. Chloroform is sometimes taken by mouth accidentally or with suicidal intent. When taken by mouth, the fatal dose would be about one and one-half ounces.

Chloroform has not been used in most hospitals or during surgeries since about the mid to late 1980s.

An abortion, when performed by a therapeutic clinic, a surgeon would determine how long the pregnancy was before establishing what actions to take to abort the child. If the pregnancy was not over a couple months, the most common use would be to thoroughly clean and sterilize the opening of the uterus and vaginal area. Then the uterus would be dilated; the fetus and after birth would be scraped out. If the pregnancy were over three months, the surgeon would probably pack the uterus with gauze.

"Criminal abortions are usually performed under conditions which would not be tolerated in a regular hospital. In the first place, the woman is not prepared for operation as she would be for a regular surgical procedure. The abortionist usually has no assistant and it is usually impossible to carry out sterile surgical techniques." according to a Homicide Investigation guideline book.

In the Rio Grande Valley, there are many *parteras,* [English: midwife] who assist in child birth and performing such abortions. There are also abortion clinics both in the Rio Grande Valley area and in the neighboring Mexico cities. There was absolutely no need for Tony to have risked Lorinda's life or that of the unborn child's - his flesh and blood.

At no time did Tony ever say that he sterilized anything when attempting to perform the abortion.

Noe Garza, a High School running buddy of Tony's, would remember that Officer Jesus Venegas had a brother named, Juan Venegas that also ran around with him and Tony. After the fire, Tony would question Juan as to what information his brother, Officer Venegas, may have or might know. Juan Venegas would only state that he did not know anything about the investigation. Mr. Garza remembered that it was almost like an obsession with Tony having to know, needing to know. Even in his youth, Tony performed damage control.

Texas Rangers met with Chief Guy Anderson and Texas Ranger Bruce Casteel at the police headquarters on November 20, 2003. After a short briefing, investigators and officials went to the Motel 6. All boundaries of room #51 had been sealed and preserved since the November 19th fire.

A report from the City of Houston Arson Bureau which was asked to assist in the investigation states, "the fire had burned itself out prior to discovery by motel employees and the discovery was made during a routine check of the room. No action of extinguishment was required by the fire department or anyone else. The victim was lying in a bed, face up, under the bed covers. There was no indication that she had tried to escape from the fire. The victim was charred from approximately the waist up (consistent with the burn pattern on the double bed). The pathologist related that she had no excess concentration of carbon monoxide in the blood. The esophagus and the trachea had indications of soot and flame; that she had no traces of drugs or alcohol."

"These investigators observed where a fire had occurred in a single occupancy motel room on the double bed. The fire originated at the head end of the bed near the left corner (when facing the bed from the foot end). The burn pattern was concentrated on the left corner and tapered to the right corner, burning a triangular shaped area approximate 2 ft. x 3 ft. . At the left corner, the fire burned through the mattress (made of rubber foam and ticking) and burned partially through the box springs. One pillow was consumed and approx. ½ of another pillow was burned. The bed was protected where the body was lying, except for the area around the head of the victim. The fire spread upwards leaving a distinct burn pattern on the sheetrock wall. This pattern was on the left side of the bed near the left corner. The burn pattern (approx. 3 ½ ft. wife) went all the way to the ceiling and spread horizontally for about 3 ft. each direction. The sheetrock wall was not damaged extensively, only burning the exposed paper on the sheetrock. The fire did not extend below the level of the mattress. The head board (formica laminated) was charred for approx. 2 ft. across the left corner. The fire did not communicate to any other item in the room, other than some burning of the drapes near the top. The accumulation of soot was very light, indicating a free burning fire."

"It is the opinion of these investigators that this is incendiary for the following reasons:

1. The burn pattern on the bed is not consistent with an accidental fire.

   A. the pattern had an irregular perimeter consistent with a liquid poured on a surface, not consistent with a smoldering fire, or a fire spread from radiated heat.

   B. the burn was about the same over the entire pattern, consistent with a liquid when ignited, not consistent with a cigarette fire, which will burn (as a smoldering fire) in a circular pattern as it expands in all directions from a specific point.

C. the fire spread across the head of the victim (both sides of the head) which should have been a temporary barrier to flame propagation. This is assuming that a fire started at a specific point.

2. The char pattern on the sheetrock wall was typical of a fast burning fire (as a flammable liquid) that is, narrow and not expanding into a fan shaped pattern.

3. There was no concentration of carbon monoxide in the blood of the victim, which is produced in large amounts by a smoldering fire, yet the windpipe had indications that the fire and smoke had been inhaled.

4. The soot produced was minimal, indicating a fast, free burning fire, not consistent with a typical smoldering fire."

"It is the opinion of these investigators (B. W. Emmons and D. R. Callaway of the Houston Arson Bureau) that an incendiary fire occurred in Room 51 and that a flammable liquid was the primary fuel; that the fire burned until the liquid was consumed. These investigators took a series of photographs of the scene and samples of the bedding that remained."

*Clarrisa, Lori's good friend, remembered that "there was so little of Lori left that I remembered her body was placed in a baby's size casket. Her funeral was at a funeral home in Kingsville and she was buried in Kingsville, that's where Mr. Rocha's family is from."

Lori was buried on November 22, 1983 in Kingsville, Texas. Turcotte-Piper Funeral Home handled the arrangements. A memorial service took place at Our Lady of Good Counsel Catholic Church on Kleberg Street in Kingsville. Lori was laid to rest at Chamberlain Cemetery, plot A West 23 C, also in Kingsville, where other members of her family are buried. All arrangements were paid for by her Father - and even with Tony's plea out - the Courts did not make a stipulation for Tony to pay any restitution.

Kingsville, Texas is just south of Corpus Christi on Highway 77, about a 30 minute drive. It is home of the renowned King Ranch, one of the oldest and largest ranches in the world. Tourist come from all over the world to visit the King Ranch visitor centers and many take the tour of the ranch, which includes imbibing in coffee with the cowpokes. There are other museums, as well as parks, in Kingsville, like the Kaufer-Hubert Memorial Park, John E. Conner Museum, Ben P. Bailey Art Building Gallery, Dick Kleberg Park, and J. K. Northway Exposition Center/Park, to name a few spots.

Kingsville came into its own being, when in 1904 the first train that included St. Louis, Brownsville and Mexico railways landed in the center of the King Ranch. Mrs. Henrietta King donated the land and was very instrumental in the settlement and growth of the area. The King family name is almost an idolized icon in the area and Texas for that matter, not only for their cattle, horses, but also for their many contributions to mankind and the City of Kingsville.

Had this "incident" happened today, Tony would or could have been charged with capital murder considering the death of a fetus was involved in Lori's murder. Tony could have been executed or be awaiting execution by now.

According the Texas Department of Criminal Justice's website marked Death Row Facts, the average time on Texas' death row is 10.43 years

Capital murder is charged when there is more than one criminal act at the time of a murder or the murder of a child under the age of 6. Most recently, in Beaumont, Texas, a man bragged when he was arrested by the Jefferson County Sheriff's Officers, "the State couldn't give me the death penalty for stuffing the kid in an oven because I waited 'til he was older than 6" according to a statement made to the media.

In Tony's case, there was arson, theft, practicing medicine without a license, theft of the drugs and the death of two - the mother and their unborn child. Modern day prosecutors would have had a field day with this case and I am quite sure there would not have been a plea bargain for arson - but a full blown trial of capital murder. And, it wouldn't have surprised me for Tony to have been given the death penalty.

Tony did go to the Harlingen police station about 10:30 AM on December 27, 1983 as requested by Captain Doster. He must have known the gig was over. Tony gave a statement, then another statement. Later his attorney, would file motions in court asking that the confessions be thrown out. Those Motions would be denied.

In my research of the original police reports, Tony lied to officers over and over. He was questioned several times as to what took place. It wasn't until he failed a polygraph test that he would later confess - after being properly read his Miranda rights.

Through Tony's own admissions in his last statement, the one taken after he failed his polygraph test in December, 1983, Tony stated, "... [I] took a 15 mg test tube of chloroform which I had with me.. While in the room Lorinda took a shower and after that we had sex. After that she lay in the bed and asked me to start with the abortion. I took a small bath towel and placed it over her nose. I told her to relax and to breathe slowly and I started dripping the chloroform into the towel which I was holding over her nose. Lorinda appeared to have gone under and I then started to open her vagina up and Lorinda started waking up and told me that I should give her more chloroform as she was feeling a little pain. I then took the same bath towel, placed it over her nose and started dripping more chloroform into it until Lorinda went under again. About that time Lorinda started breathing heavily and I started to recognize some symptoms ….I realized at that time that Lorinda had taken too much chloroform and I began to panic…. I really started to panic. I sat down beside her and started crying. I tried to relax but I could not, I lighted a marijuana joint while I was sitting beside her. I sat there smoking ….I put one of her cigarettes into her hand and lit it as I wanted it to look like an accident. Her hand holding the cigarette was lying by the pillow and a fire started slowly on the pillow and all of a sudden the pillow just blazed up. I just sat there in the chair watching the fire spread. The fire then started burning the blanket and smoke and heat was too much for me to stand. .. So I went outside and drove around. I drove back to the hospital about 10:45 PM or 11:00 PM …."

Clarissa's statement regarding Tony being brutal to Lori during their sexual encounters was consistent with Tony's confession of having had sex just prior to his attempt to abort the baby and Officer Venegas' report of finding blood under her when her charred body was removed from the bed.

Tony wrote to the Cameron County District Clerk, in Brownsville, Texas, after he was sent to prison and even in a letter Tony sent to Judge Hester during his incarceration prior to taking a plea bargain of a lesser charge of Arson, Tony did not take responsibility for his actions, nor does he accept responsibility today for Lori and his unborn child's murder.

Tony wrote, "I am innocent of the charges they have charge[d] me with. You will hear my side of the truth when the trial is due. I am a fun loving person with everyone, and also a professional in my field….I have been in jail for five months and have hated every day of these weeks. I don't belong here sir with these people…..I am going crazy here. I want to be with my family I love them very much. I've had a minister visit me every Saturday and time I tell him I'm losing a part of myself every day here…"

Mr. Abel Cavada, the attorney who represented Tony at one of his hearings, made this statement, "I worked all over the valley. I am an independent person involved in politics from the past and I used to get a lot of cases that people would refer to me. I received a phone call from some farm worker ladies who were friends to the father and who went to the dad's [Mr. Gonzales Sr.] church. I believe he had a small Pentecostal church in San Benito. This guy [Tony] was given a young new lawyer [at first] and during a bond reduction hearing the attorney opened the door and had a full hearing, which you aren't suppose to do - just suppose to talk about the finances. The guy [attorney] blew it and Tony gave a lot of admissions [during the hearing]. So the dad hired me and I took over the case. I have degrees in psychology and after taking Tony to the crime scene, I knew he was a sociopath, because he had no conscience. Initially, I thought Tony would flip out or something when he got to the scene, but he didn't. He just stood there cold and started pointing things out as to what happened and where everything was, like he was analyzing things. He wasn't affected at all by the crime scene. The next day, I and the investigator picked him up to make sure he got to court on time and we had the radio turned down real low. Tony heard a song that he liked and said "hey turn that up." So I did. I look in the back seat and on the way to court there he is dancing in the back seat. I found that very strange. I went to Cantu who was the DA at the time and asked about a plea bargain. Cantu said that if Tony didn't take the plea bargain that Cantu was going to ask the Judge to reset the hearing and Cantu was going to re-indict him for capital murder because she was alive when he burned her. So, that's why I convinced Tony to take the 60 years and then Cantu wouldn't re-indict him. This is probably one of the worse cases I have ever been involved in."

Mr. Cavada went on to say, "At one point the girl, Lorinda, went to another state, Tennessee to be with her grandparents - I think her parents knew what type of guy Tony really was and thought they knew about the sex and all so they sent her to get her away from Tony.

After about a month or so, she flew back to Harlingen and paged Tony at his job to come get her at the airport. He took one of the girl's girlfriends with him to pick her up. Instead of taking her home, they went to a park on U.S. 77. There he started performing oral sex on her in front of the girlfriend who freaked out and went running into the woods. A couple of days later is when Tony killed the girl."

Perhaps, Mr. Cavada is not far off in his assessment that Tony was cold. When Tony was chewed out for doing things that could easily violate his parole, Tony would not say a word, then abruptly say, "I've gotta go" and leave without retorting or responding back to what had just been said.

Eileena, a girlfriend Tony acquired after he was released from prison, called him a "murderer" and a "baby killer". Tony would sit there, never flinch a muscle, never show any emotion, and would just continue on as if nothing had been said.

Tony gave up the right to say he was innocent when on April 30, 1984 in the 197th Judicial District Court in Cameron County, Brownsville, Texas Courtroom with his attorney, Mr. Abel Cavada, of Victoria, Texas, whom Tony's parents had hired for him, he, and the State prosecutor, Tony pled guilty to Count Four of the indictment - Arson. The court transcript, Volume 63 Page 123 states: "...the Defendant had a right to withdraw his plea and his judicial admission of guilt before the Court and any matters discussed or written in the probation report would not be used against him, but the Defendant persisted in pleading guilty. It plainly appearing to the Court that the Defendant is mentally competent and that his plea is free and voluntary the said plea was by the Court received and is now entered upon the Minutes of the Court as the plea herein of said Defendant. Thereupon, the Defendant, in person in open court, having waived the right of trial by jury in writing, requested the Court to approve the waiver of jury. The Court then determined that such waiver in writing, signed by the Defendant, had been filed herein before the Defendant entered his plea of guilty and that the attorney representing the State had consented in writing to such waiver. The consent and approval of the Court for the Defendant to waive the right of trial by jury was then granted."

"Whereupon, the Defendant proceeded to trial before the Court, who having heard and considered the pleadings and evidence offered, is of the opinion therefrom, and so finds, that the Defendant is guilty of the offense of Arson, as set out in Count Four of the Indictment, which offense was committed on November 18, 1983, in Cameron County, Texas."

"It is, therefore, considered and adjudged by the Court that the Defendant, Jose Antonio Gonzalez, Jr., is guilty of the offense of Arson as charged in the Fourth Count of the Indictment as confessed by him in his plea of guilty herein made......the Defendant be punished by confinement in the Texas Department of Corrections for a period of sixty (60) years and that the State of Texas do have and recover of the said Defendant all costs in this prosecution expended, for which execution will issue."

"And thereupon, the Defendant, Jose Antonio Gonzalez, Jr., was asked by the Court whether he had anything to say why said sentence should not be pronounced against him, and he answered nothing in bar thereof. Whereupon, the Court proceeded, in the presence of the said Defendant, Jose Antonio Gonzalez, Jr., to pronounce sentence.... punishment has been assessed by the Court at confinement in the Texas Department of Corrections for a term of sixty (60) years, be delivered by the Sheriff of Cameron County, Texas immediately to the Director of Corrections of the Texas Department of Corrections ..."

I knew Tony would not tell the truth to anyone in Beaumont or to his parents, just like it took well over six weeks back in 1983 for him to admit what he had done to Lorinda and their baby.

Even today, Tony tells people that his prison stint was all Lorinda's fault. Her family and friends have a different opinion, as do many of Tony's family and acquaintances.

*Clarissa said "Lori was my best friend. We lived not far from each other. I was younger than she, but she was still my best friend. She was beautiful. Unfortunately I only have 3 photos of Lori - I guess back then we didn't take many pictures."

Clarissa went on to say, "In my opinion Tony is a worthless piece of shit son-of-bitch. He should have burned. I do know at times, it was like Lori was under a spell with him."

After the death of her daughter and Tony's sentencing, on May 31, 1984, Mrs. Beverly Rocha wrote to Mr. & Mrs. Gonzalez, Senior. She wrote:

*"Dear Mr. & Mrs. Gonzales,*

*Although we have never met, I had to write to you. I am Lori Rocha's mother. She spoke of you often I have heard from many people that you are very nice.*

*I am sorry for the way things turned out for our children. They both had only started their lives - God willing, your son will return to you and begin a new life.*

*I want you and Tony, Jr. to know that I do not have any hate in my heart for him. I feel only sadness for what he did and sorrow for what he must endure.*

*You, your other children and Tony will always be remembered in my prayers. Please tell Tony to obey all rules and go to the Lord with his problems.*

*God Bless you all,*
*Beverly Rocha"*

21

Mrs. Rocha has to be one of the kindest, most compassionate people in the world. I do not believe, that as a mother, I could have done this. But, then again, this act of kindness must have been the beginning of her healing - if there is such a thing in losing a child, so young and so tragic.

Because I wanted to give Tony the benefit of the doubt and help the guy out, I asked *Tom Tucker, an attorney friend of mine who was doing parole packets at the time to do one for Tony. Tom Tucker prepared a parole packet for Tony.

During the time that Tom. Tucker was working on the parole packet, I was working other investigations. I own LinMarie Garsee & Associates, a private investigations firm in Beaumont, Texas. During this time, I made a couple of trips to the Rio Grande Valley of Texas working on another case - a death penalty Writ of Habeas Corpus.

While in the Rio Grande Valley of Texas, I made what would be my first trip to meet with Tony's parents, Tony, Sr. and Catalina Gonzalez. I told Tony's parents that the parole packet needed as many letters of support for Tony from as many people as possible. I was assured by Mr. & Mrs. Gonzalez that they would get the letters and get them to me as soon as quickly as they could. Tony had said "do not tell my parents anything about my business, I do not like my parents and they blame me for my Sister's death."

My initial visit with Tony's parents went well. They lived in a modest wood framed house at the end of South C Street near the drainage ditch. At that time, there were no screens on the door or windows, the couch was covered with a blanket that was attempting to cover up the springs that were piercing through the thread worn cushions. The carpet on the floor was pretty much worn to where you could see the backing on the carpet.

There were babies there. Tony's 15 year old niece lived there with her 2 children and husband, as did Mr. & Mrs. Gonzalez. It was a typical site in the Valley. Babies having babies, several generations living under the same roof, barren yards where little to no grass grew. Poor but proud.

The kitchen consisted of a small 1950's style dining table with an inlaid top and plastic covered metal chairs - three, I recall.

Tony, Sr. did the talking. Catalina seemed to be the typical South Texas subservient wife, who did what the man of the house said to do. I felt there was much more that she would have liked to have said, but didn't. Tony, Sr. was eager for his son to make up for the years that he had lost, to find a wife, settle down and have children. I told him Tony thought that Tony, Sr. blamed Tony for the death of his Sister, Cindy. To which Tony, Sr. responded, "No way."

But, having seen the babies, the thought that Tony and Lorinda's child would have been welcomed by this family crossed my mind, as I was sure that Lorinda's family would have loved and cared for the baby as well. Perhaps it was God's whispers telling me to look at the situation again- but I didn't listen.

From all accounts, Tony, Sr. was a very hard working man. He owns his own painting business and had aspirations of Tony coming back to Harlingen and working with him. Tony, on the other hand, wanted nothing to do with neither his Dad's business nor his Dad. In one letter written to me, Tony wrote this regarding his family, "it's been years since I saw any of my family. I do not know who they are and they do not know who I am."

Perhaps these living conditions even fortified my desire to do something positive in Tony's life and help him obtain and keep his freedom with parole, by giving him a better place to live, a better life style than what he would have in the Rio Grande Valley and from the sound of things from him - that he never had.

I made a second trip to Harlingen in the latter part of 2001, at the behest of Tom Tucker to obtain more information from the Tony's parents. I phoned Catalina and requested that she go to Brownsville and get me a complete copy of Tony's file from the courthouse. I told her exactly where we were to meet, there in Harlingen. I was down there with two of my investigators and a friend doing a job for an 11.071 Writ.

Patricia Olney was sick that day and stayed at the hotel. I'd asked the hotel clerk that if anyone came in looking or asking for me to please direct them to Mrs. Olney's room. Tony's parents never showed up at the hotel.

When I tried to call the Tony's parents, there was no answer. Tony would later tell Reggie Johnson, and anyone who would listen, that "my Brother and Mother waited for her at the store with all that paper work and she never showed up." Even though, a few days later, Catalina called and said she hadn't gotten the paper work and couldn't make it to the hotel meeting.

I came back to Beaumont empty handed and ended up contracting a private investigations firm from Brownsville to get the information needed. I paid almost $800 to get the information that Mr. Tucker needed to be used in Tony's parole packet. Tony stated "I will pay you back for this, I promise."

At one point, Fred Power, a friend of mine, and me made a trip to Harlingen to pick up the letters of support that Tony's parents had gathered from his family, friends and business associates in support of Tony getting out. When we pulled up to the house, Fred wouldn't even get out - he was in shock that people lived like that.

Fred said, "Just leave the truck running. I am not getting out and going anywhere near that house." Fred didn't get out of the truck. I didn't stay long; I was inside the house just long enough to gather up the letters.

Fred's impression of the living conditions and the house was "actually it was almost frightening I just felt very uncomfortable. It was pretty pretty bad, really." Fred would ask me, "Don't you remember that character that came out of the house without any doors on the front of it?" And, yes, I did remember.

He reminded me that some years earlier, perhaps 1986 or so, that a satanic cult had kidnapped a young man, Mark Kilroy, from Hitchcock, Texas, who was visiting the Rio Grande Valley while on Spring Break and crossed over the Rio Grande River into Matamoras, Mexico, the city just opposite Brownsville. His body was found among others at a satanic ritual site. To those living in Mexico, such rituals are not unheard of, in fact, they are an excepted part of life to many.

I am not suggesting that Tony's parents are like that cult, nor, to my knowledge, do they have anything to do with such. In fact, to my knowledge, they are praying parents. But, being in a different culture and a different lifestyle than what Fred and I were accustomed to, initially, not knowing what, nor who was going to greet me, was a spooky feeling - especially in light of Tony's remarks about how his Dad "would beat them regularly."

In one letter just prior to his release, Tony wrote, "I wrote {my parents} a long letter explaining why I wasn't going to the Valley and she [his mother] is fishing about what I'm going to do when I get out!! But go ahead and send the money this way. Part of me says, "no," then I do think, "why not take it?" I do still think about at times of their blaming me for my Sister's death. That's why I haven't call[ed] I guess. I had a lot of questions when she died and no one answered them. Left in the dark, still that way, don't know anything really enough of that."

The letters of support that Tony received all alluded to great respect to Tony, Sr.. Many letters described how both families had suffered.

Being a small, close-knit community, everyone pretty much knew everyone and their parents and grandparents.

One supporter wrote: "…[I] have know[n] Jose Antonio Gonzalez Sr. for about thirty years. He is a nice person and a hardworking man. I'm certain if his son Jose Antonio Gonzalez Jr. is paroled he would be a good asset to the community."

The letter was written based on the Tony, Sr.'s reputation. Many who wrote letters only knew Tony as a "little boy" or "he was so young when this all happened."

Another support letter said, "[Tony] comes from a very good family and I would certainly expect him to be a good citizen if allowed to return to Harlingen."

And, another wrote, "I have known Jose Antonio Gonzalez, Sr. for approximately fifteen years. Tony, Sr. has painted both my home and my mother's home many times. He is known in this community for his quality workmanship and friendly way of doing business. Although I do not know Tony, Jr. … ."

The majority of the letters were written in support of Tony's family, trying to show what close family ties there are between the son and his family. But, was that all an illusionary dream of his family's? Why after over 3 years now, has Tony not gone home to visit his parents or they him?

I had an inside scoop of when things were going to happen at the prison. One of the female guards that Tony was "friends" with, called me at my house several times at night from her home phone to pass messages for him. Tony also had an inside source, an inmate, to let him know from a computer inside the prison when the Board of Pardons and Parole made their decision. Tony knew he was going to be paroled before his own attorney knew!

The minute that Tony wrote that he had gotten his F-1 (a rating that the Board of Pardons and Parole gives when classifying an inmate for release) I told him to pack up his things in the craft shop. Tony did listen to me. Charles "Charlie" Ryan was on Tony's visitation list. Charlie went up to the Wynne Unit and picked up all of Tony's belongings because I had warned Tony to pack up if he wanted to make sure that he got everything. Tony wrote me saying "everyone said you don't know what you are talking about and I am a fool for packing things up."

A few days later I received a letter from Tony stating, "MeMe, [LinMarie] I am so glad that I listened to you - I am being shipped to pre-release today. I will write you to let you know where I am being sent to when I get there." We were all excited! I phoned Tony's parents, even though Tony had asked me not to, to let them know what was happening.

Tony's mother, Catalina, cried with joy. I am a Mother and I respected her as Tony's Mother. Mothers need to know positive things about their children, no matter how old they get. Mothers need to know the good and the bad; and, we love our children no matter what comes between us.

Tony's truck load of belongings stayed locked up in storage for over a year in my garage. I had no idea what was in there, nor did I care to discover anything until Tony came home and showed it to us.

A few days later, Tony wrote a letter from a pre-release unit in Mineral Wells, Texas. Mineral Wells is in north central Texas, west of Fort Worth.

The last year that Tony was in the pre-release unit, I pretty much supported him. I bought clothes for both winter and summer for Tony and sent them to him. And, according to Tony, "the clothes have got to be monogrammed with my name on it or some marking so that it can distinguish that they are mine." I didn't have a sewing machine that would monogram.  For each piece of clothing, I paid $12.50 to monogram Tony's name on to the clothes;  and also  paid the UPS postage to get it to him. I sent money for Tony to "eat" on. Having heard the horror stories from Tony and other inmates of the food servings or lack thereof , I knew that Tony would want to buy food.  And, many times inmates share a "spread" with the other guys.

A "spread" in prison terms is similar to a picnic.  Everyone puts something in that is purchased at the commissary (or stolen contraband from those who work in the kitchens, like boiled eggs or onions or anything else that might spice up the evening) and even the poor ones who have no commissary money are included - especially during the holidays or by the most benevolent  who may be participating.

I also included Tony in plans to be a  partner with Two Hearts Leather, Silver & More.  However,  Tony only lasted about a month working in the store when he got out.  After Tony's departure, I renamed the store and the Corporation to protect the partners  and me.

In fact, in Tony's parole packet, it shows that Tony had a job waiting on him - with us!  Though, Tony  was not going to be "manager of a craft store" as was published, he was going to work as a clerk and manufacturer silver items.  Each partner would have a role.  Prior to his release, Tony was put on the checking account as a full partner.

Our initial stock of leather and silver was extremely low.  I purchased leather items from other leather workers.  Tony was to have had a lot of his silver already prepared.  However, as I was soon to learn, he didn't. This, too, should have been another red flag of what the future with Tony  may hold.

During the time that Tony was at the  pre-release unit, many plans were made.  Tony phoned at least 2-3 times a week.  At $14.00 a call, that quickly added up over the course of 12 months. And, of course in almost every letter, he would write, "MeMe, [LinMarie] I am going to pay you back for all of those phone calls. I know they are expensive and you have other bills and things to pay."

Part of the agreement between the partners was that Tony were going to do hauling and yard work, with Tony mowing grass around the house with the push mower.

In many letters Tony wrote, "I will do all of the work like that . I will do it. It is the least I can do for what ya'll are doing for me." This decision and work was to help be able to buy stock, increase advertising, get out of the debt that had been incurred thus far in the business and to prepare for a future.

Tony would later write, "I will pay you back every dime for what you've helped me." Those were famous last words - if anything, Tony got me more into debt.

And, there was the, "[LinMarie] I will flip burgers to help make money to get the things we need and make our business a success. I'll work two jobs. " However, that was another lie. Because upon his release, I introduced Tony to a friend who was a manager at the local Whataburger. She offered him a job. Tony turned it down, stating, "I'm not about to flip burgers, I have a college degree!"

I would also learn that Tony's college "degree" was why he wouldn't go back to his family in the Rio Grande Valley and "lower himself to be among his family and do slave labor for his Dad". Even though in his statement to the Parole Board Tony stated, "….[I] wish to get reacquainted with my family and begin saving money. I am not married but hopefully that will change….My vision cannot come true without having God in the picture. With His help I will succeed."

To this date, over three years has passed and Tony has yet to go to see his parents. He supposedly speaks to them by telephone every Sunday.

On a visit with Catalina, on November 19, 2004, she asked, "what does my son [Tony] look like?" Tony has a camera - he was given plenty of photos of himself when he lived with us, surely, he cannot be so self-consumed and heartless not to at least send his parents a photo of himself- but then again - maybe he is, or she would not have asked me that question. Upon my return home, I sent Catalina some photos that were taken the day that Tony came to Beaumont from the pre-release unit.

I've often said, that no matter what our children do to us, as parents, we still love them, still believe them and in them and we still only want the very best for them and we probably will protect them as long as we have a breathe in us. I can see from the family values of the Hispanic culture, Tony's parents being just that way.

While incarcerated, Tony attended Lee College, in 1996 and earned an Associate of Applied Science Degree in 1996, Lee College in 1987 for Electronics Technology and just prior to his release was presently attending Sam Houston State University towards receiving a Bachelor of Science Degree. Had Tony not only gotten a college education, but also a Ph.D. in "conning"? That was a question that would haunt me for a long time.

Knowing that Tony would be lost as to how Harlingen had grown, one of Tony's and Lorinda's friends, Bettina (Anzaldua) Elliott worked with me putting together photos of old friends and the Harlingen. I paid for the photos and the shipping - just trying to do whatever I could to get things together that would make Tony feel comfortable and make his transition as smoothly as possible. These were put into his leather photo album that he had received as a gift on his first night "home".

Tony would write, "I wrote my friend [Bettina] and told her why I would never go back to the [Rio Grande] Valley." Bettina doesn't remember getting such a letter.

Tony arrived in Beaumont, Texas, on March 1, 2002 at 7:35pm. Earlier that morning he had phoned me from a pay phone outside a small convenience store there in Mineral Wells, Texas, where he was waiting for his bus that would "bring him home". Tony had cashed his check (money left from his trust fund), bought himself some snacks and was waiting for the bus driver to call for everyone to board the bus. When Tony arrived in Beaumont, Dee Bailey, Janice Reynolds, Reggie Johnson, Donald Paul Stricklan (who worked for us at the store), and others were there. We had made posters welcoming him home. None of these people knew Tony. They were there at my behest, they were my friends, who wanted to give Tony support and make him feel welcome.

Someone on the bus with him said, "Wow, someone's getting a welcome home." Tony reported that when he looked out and saw it was his "family" he told those on the bus, "oh it's for me!" A girl responded, "I wish my Mom would give me a welcome like that!"

We all headed to the house where Tony had a party waiting for him. We had a large pot of seafood gumbo - just what he'd asked for. And, there were gifts. Lots of photos were taken, which would later be added to the other photos inside the photo album where the photos of Harlingen - familiar faces and places - of things and people that he'd not seen in over eighteen years were carefully placed.

We gave him the leather photo album, a roper wallet (his choice), he was given clothes, shoes, a belt - and in his room - he had 15 shirts, 20 each undershirts & underwear & socks, 10 pairs of blue jeans, jackets, cologne, deodorant, toothbrush . . . It was as if he'd always lived there and he wanted for nothing... including something that he'd asked for - a Bible - because he was going to go to church with us. Tony's going to church with us occurred one time. Tony remarked, "This church stuff ain't for me."

Among the goals Tony wrote in his parole packet presented to the Texas Board of Pardons and Paroles was, "My goals are to report to my parole office/pay my fees on time; Maintain status of law-abiding, productive citizen; Successfully complete parole requirements and stipulations; Re-establish relationship with family; Rebuild and maintain my life; Set a good example for others; Help my family and friends in any way I can; Work and establish myself; Attend and participate in church and/or community activities; and Be an asset to my community."

Whatever Tony asked for - he got. And, after I developed the photos, I put everything into a scrapbook and decorated them up for him.

Tony made a few phone calls to people in the Rio Grande Valley - but none to his parents. One call Tony made was to a lady he had worked with at Valley Baptist Hospital. She was married and had befriended Tony after he went to prison and "felt sorry for him that he got into that trouble, but I even felt sorrier for the girl and her family."

Two weeks later, Tony's friend Bettina Anzaldua and her fiancé, Tim Elliott came for a crawfish boil - sort of a belated welcome home party with someone from his past. Bettina and Tim were married a few months later.

On Saturday evening, we all went to First Baptist Church's Passion Play at the Julie Rogers Center in downtown Beaumont. This presentation is a bi-annual production put on by the church about the life, death and resurrection of Jesus. The sound and lighting effects were awesome. Tony kept commenting on how much he enjoyed it. We all had enjoyed it.

At first I didn't know how to accept Bettina. She was flamboyant, loud, and had a strange laugh. But, the more you are around her, you learn that she is the most loving, caring, forgiving, non-judgmental and understanding person in the world. I can see how, over the years, she had continued to befriend Tony after he had killed Lorinda and their unborn child.

I cleaned house after everyone left - Tony watched TV. Odd, that wasn't the way it was supposed to be. But that was the way it was.

I was often puzzled about what the relationship between Tony and Bettina or "BT" as Tony called her was.

She would explain it this way, " 'BT' is a name people used to call me when I was in school. It was either that or 'Betty' & I sure don't think I'm a 'Betty'. I hate that name. I don't like 'BT' much either so I don't use it. Just a few people like Chris still call me that. Mainly 'beauty shop' people since I was a hair stylist."

After over 3 years, lots of visits with Bettina and Tim both in the Rio Grande Valley at their home, the home of her parents, Joe and Isabelle Anzaldua, and here in Beaumont at my home, Bettina gave me this explanation of the relationship between her and Tony and her becoming aware of Lori's death, Tony's arrest and incarceration:

*"... by accident, I stumbled across an article one November afternoon on an inside page of the Valley Morning Star with the headline something to the effect of "Woman found burned in motel". Somewhat startled, I sat down to read the story. This was how I learned that Lori Rocha had died.*

*I read the story twice, once quickly, scanning for details, then slowly, focusing on each word in the short article. I was having trouble focusing however, thru the shock that comes in reading that a friend had died. My first thought was, "Oh God, they're gonna be looking for Tony."*

*Not that I had any idea Tony could possibly be capable of any involvement in something as horrible as this, but I knew he had dated Lori & I had seen enough TV cop shows to know you always start*

with a spouse or "significant other" when there is a death. I knew
Tony would be questioned. I wondered if I would be as well because
everyone knew Tony and I were very close.

I met Lori thru Tony, when they started dating in high school. She
was so cute, very petite & always smiling. They made a great couple.
Tony wasn't too tall so they looked like they were made for each
other. They seemed to get along well. She [Lori] didn't come across, at
least to me, as a jealous or possessive girl friend, which I appreciated
because Tony and I had been friends for about 4 years by that time.

I started cutting Lori's hair at this time as I was already a licensed
cosmetologist by the time I was sixteen.

"Ironically, when the story broke about Lori, I had just watched
a TV show on, of all things, "Spontaneous Human Combustion".
Within a few days of reading the article, I called Tony and we made
plans to have lunch at a local restaurant, the Lone Star.

"I didn't waste any time. I asked right away If the police had come
to see him about Lori's death. He said they had talked to him but he
told them he didn't know anything. He was talking kind of fast.  I
could tell he was nervous, but I couldn't blame him."

"After all, who is calm when the police are asking you about
your involvement in a murder? I didn't feel that Tony was trying to
cover up anything. I certainly didn't think he would be lying to me. I
mean, come on, I couldn't really be sitting here with someone who is
responsible for another persons death. Especially someone I trusted
and loved dearly."

"We talked about the TV show. He said, "That's probably what
happened to Lori. I told the cops I don't know anything." He kept
repeating that last part seven or eight  times during our conversation."

"I told him I immediately thought of him [Tony] when I read it
because they [Tony and Lori]  had dated. I even said to him "like you

would ever hurt anyone, Tony." I never knew Tony to be mean, cruel or insensitive to anyone. I saw him as such a caring, compassionate young man. I used to tell him he was gonna make such a good father and husband some day. He said he was very much looking forward to that, but later, much later.

"When the story broke about Tony being arrested in Lori's death, I was devastated. I didn't want to talk about it. I didn't want to read the paper, nothing. This had to be a mistake. Something had gone horribly wrong and they had the wrong guy."

"Someone, maybe Noe [Garza], told me Juan Venegas' brother [Jesus Venegas] was one of the investigators working on the case. I called Juan. We talked for a few hours. By now, I guess Tony had begun to tell a little of what really happened that day at Motel 6."

"Juan mentioned something about "murder one", or "premeditated murder" & I really freaked out. It was like the air was sucked out of me How could I know someone capable of this? How could someone I trust be in jail for murder? Who was going to be my best friend now? "

"I guess he got out on bail or something, because a little bit later, my mom and sisters were at the mall and they saw Tony, or someone who looked just like him, walk by them in the food court going to the movies with a girl. They looked right at him and he just kept walking."

"I called Tony's house that night. His sister, Cindy answered. I said, "Hi Cindy, it's BT, can I speak w/ Tony?" I heard muffled sounds, like the receiver was covered, then they hung up the phone. I called back a few minutes later & no one answered. After Tony was sent to Huntsville, he wrote to me and apologized for that incident. He said they had lots of "crank calls" during all that trial stuff, etc. and they just started hanging up. "

"Tony was really good about answering letters. If I wrote, he'd answer. If I didn't write, he wouldn't either. He told me he didn't want to be an imposition on my life. By that time, I had gotten married and he didn't want to do anything that could possibly cause any problems in my marriage."

"Actually, for the 15 months I lived overseas, I didn't write for that very reason. All mail was delivered to "the unit". My husband saw every piece of mail we got first. I knew he would start accusing me of trying to maintain some sort of romantic relationship with "my boyfriend". (He was extremely insecure & immature when it came to anything regarding me and anyone who was my friend, male or female.)"

"In his letters, Tony told of how he had been made a trustee and was attending college. Wanting to facilitate his correspondence, I sent some self addressed stamped envelopes, not knowing this was completely against the rules of TDC. They were sent back to me with a letter explaining that nothing could be sent in and if I desired, I could make a deposit in the inmate trust fund. "

"They included one little slip stating that was contraband and he wrote to me too and said he had to go in a[nd] sign some papers concerning that incident too. He assured me it was ok, that he hadn't gotten into any trouble or anything. He also sent me several of the inmate trust fund slips and asked if I could make the smallest deposit.

"Truly, I wished I could have, but I absolutely had zero to spare. He never mentioned it again. I kept the slips for years in my stationary box. I always meant to make a small deposit, even $5. [But I didn't]"

"For years, I kept most of the letters Tony sent me. I'm not sure why. Periodically, I'd read them. I had trouble deciphering his handwriting sometimes, but I could hear his voice in my head as I'd read the letters. He sounded the same. His spirit seemed to be intact."

*"Often, he would tell me how he spends his time reading in the library & studying. I encouraged him to keep attending classes." "When Tony was convicted and sentenced, I had again spoken with Juan Venegas and I had understood Juan to say Tony received "six years" in prison for arson."*

*"I had misunderstood what Juan had said. Many years later, like 10 years, I learned, while at jury duty, that the conviction was for "arson & murder" and the sentence was 60 years."* Bettina Elliott had e-mailed me.

An inmate is required to have a job that he works at for a minimum of 40 hours a week at one of the many industries within the prison system. Many people in the free world do not believe that inmates have to work. That simply is a farce that the system would like the public to believe and the myth is escalated by the media.

There are several hundreds of industries within the prison system. All of the industries are money makers for the prison system. I suppose that is why, when I hear from the media that the Texas Prison System is financially unstable, I laugh. How could that be, unless someone is scamming off of the top; especially in light of the free labor from the inmates that the prison system uses?

Tony was no different than any other inmate on a "farm" or "unit". He had a couple of jobs while incarcerated. One, was working in the commissary and the other, was as a trustee in the craft shops. His craft shop supervisor is the one who phoned me from her home at night to give me messages from Tony. At the time of his release from the Wynne Unit in Huntsville, Texas, he was a Trustee Class III.

Being a Trustee gave Tony a lot of freedom to move around the unit - more so than an inmate who did not have that classification. He maintained a clear disciplinary record - which it has been hinted that to have a clear record in prison - one may be a snitch.

A prison snitch is protected by the person [correctional officer] that he works for, while turning over to the supervisor or warden information that may be floating around that would be against the rules of that unit. Tony had only two minor cases - which were overlooked because of their trivial nature.

Classifications are something that are earned. Tony did have rules and regulations that he had to abide by. There are many phases of classifications. With Tony's classification, he was housed in a dorm rather than a small-two-man cell or cell block. Everyone in the Rio Grande Valley area who knew Tony or Lorinda were still curious, as to what happened in 1983 and why? Perhaps in writing this book - the truth *will* come to light.

Tony's parole packet information regarding the "incident" went like this: ".....the fact situation surrounding his incarceration is much more involved than that. He has been a model inmate for 16 years and TDCJ has done its job of both punishment and rehabilitation..... ". "The incident which brought about Jose Antonio Gonzalez' incarceration goes back to 1983 in Harlingen, Texas, his childhood home, which is located in the southern most part of Texas commonly referred to as the "Rio Grande Valley". It has been predominantly populated by the Hispanic community partly due to the geographic location. These people from "The Valley" are a people of strong family ties, Old World culture, devoutly practiced Catholic religion, high morals, good standards, and strong work ethic. It is a close knit community of family and friends who cling to each other, their faith, and their culture, dignity, honor and pride. These people have lived together for generations through good times and bad. Their family ties and friendships are everlasting. This is where Lorinda Rocha and Tony grew up and where their families remain to this day."

"Lorinda and Tony grew up together and had known each other all of their lives. Prior to the incident, they had been romantically involved, but it did not last. However, shortly after their romantic involvement ended, Lorinda informed Tony she was pregnant, but that she did not want to go forth with the pregnancy. She was 18 and he was 22. The social pressures and shame brought on by being a young, unwed pregnant girl from a good family was a devastating blow. She [Lori] just couldn't face it and did not want this baby. Being as how Tony worked in a hospital, she [Lori] felt that he could help her terminate the pregnancy. She [Lorinda] was desperate and insistent up on him [Tony] helping her with it. In a fit of youthful ignorance, accelerated by the fear that Lorinda would go forth with her threats of trying to perform a self-abortion with a coat hanger, or commit suicide he [Tony] went to her thinking he could stop her from doing something terrible to herself. She [Lorinda] checked into a motel room and called Tony to come help her. He [Tony] went to her [Lorinda] and tried to administer chloroform to Lorinda, but [he] didn't do it right and couldn't put her under. He [Tony] wouldn't continue with what she wanted him to do. This ordeal terribly frightened Tony and he hoped that Lorinda would not call upon him again, but she did. Again, she [Lori] threatened a coat hanger abortion or suicide and convinced Tony to meet her at a motel and go forth with performing an abortion. Again fearing what she [Lori] might do, Tony went to her and took some chloroform. This time, things went terribly wrong. Tony administered the chloroform and in doing so, thought he had killed her. She [Lori] did not appear to be breathing. He [Tony] panicked and set the motel room on fire as he thought he had just killed her and wanted to die then and there with her. When the heat became so intense, Tony was driven from the room. He thought he would die from smoke inhalation before he would be driven from the room, but that didn't work either. He fled, not knowing what to do in a state of panic and shock. Afterwards, he [Tony] was arrested and in eventuality sent to prison for arson."

No where in the statement does Tony admit that he had stolen the chloroform -not once but twice - from the hospital where he worked. No where in the statement does Tony admit that he didn't want any kids; no where in the statement does he admit that he convinced Lori to have an abortion.

In 2002 upon his arrival in Beaumont, Texas, after being released from the pre-release unit, Tony was going to work in the store, Two Hearts, on certain days and on the days that he didn't work the store, he would work on his silver in the studio or garage.

That plan never came to fruition. Tony wanted to stay up all hours of the night and day watching television and horror movies. This led to several heated discussions about respecting others that live in the house.

Tony asked if he could play around with the computer. I said "sure, but do not go to any sex sites." Tony assured me he wouldn't. But the day after Tony used the computer I started getting all sorts of pornographic stuff sent to me on the e-mail that I had never in all of the years of using the internet received.

I asked Tony, "Did you go to any sex sites on my computer." He lied and responded, "Oh no, you said not to, so I didn't."

I later learned that Tony boasted to them that he had gone into different sex sites and he wasn't about to tell me any differently. Tony knew I was livid over receiving those nasty e-mails. I had never gotten them before, because I had never been to those sites, so I knew Tony was lying to me. It took 2 years me to learn the truth about what Tony did on my computer.

I also found out that Tony was looking for "swingers" and had asked an older friend of mine to help him find a group. *Bo being in his late 60's thought it was funny, but did not offer any help to Tony. Bo wasn't a swinger and knew nothing about any of that.

During the last four months that Tony lived in my house, he would sneak out of the house (or so he thought - we knew when the door opened) at night and walk over to Mike's on Irving Street. That was one place that I told him he had better stay away from unless he was looking for trouble.

Mike's is a drive-in grocery, run by folks who appear to be oblivious about the drug trafficking or prostituting that goes on around there. The police have made many arrests at that locale.

I had run that negative element away from my neighborhood when I first bought my house in 1992 and I surely didn't want it back. There was no way I'd ever leave my house alone with Tony for fear that he'd bring that trash to my house. In fact, in 1995, for my efforts of cleaning up my neighborhood, I won the prestigious Jefferson Award. The award was designed by Jacquelyn Kennedy Onassis in honor of those who had bettered their community. And, the events that led up to winning the award are part of my first book, Taking Back My Streets.

Within the first week of Tony being "at home", there was a problem with a guy from Baytown, who'd been incarcerated in the pre-release unit in Mineral Wells with Tony . I think his name was Padillo. The guy was suppose to have "tools that you [Tony] can have" (after Tony had "given the guy lots of food, etc."). Tony called him. The man didn't return the call. Tony called the mother of the man who said the man didn't live there and evidently had done something and she didn't want him there any more. She gave Tony the phone number of one of the man's daughter's where he was staying.

There ended up being a huge cursing fight between Tony, the daughter & the man - to the point - that there were threats made by the woman that Tony was harassing them. I phoned the police in Beaumont and explained that we were getting lots of phone calls from these people and that there were major threats taking place.

There was one more call after that, the girl calling back to call me and Tony "lying m…f…s" Again, that should have been another clue or a "God whisper" as to what I was dealing with.

In June, 2002, the three of us - Jesse, Tony, and me - took Charlie Ryan to Houston for his birthday. We went to the Museum of Natural Sciences, saw an IMAX, went to Spanish Flower to eat and then drove to Kemah to see the sights. Tony didn't pay his way, even with him having a pocket full of money.

He did, however, make Charlie a nice letter opener from deer horn [that a friend had given me] as a birthday gift. There were photos taken and three sets made so that Tony got his set of photos as well.

Later that month, we took Tony over to the zoo for a picnic and to meet one of his friends - or someone we later learned he'd met at the Mineral Wells pre-release place as well. We spent half a day there and came home. Once again two sets of photos were made and Tony got his - once more for free. I was not impressed with the friend at all.

Sometime during these summer months, Tony was mowing the property over at 1885 Park Street with the push mower. He came back over to the house where we were working on our own projects and pitched a fit and made the comment "that he wasn't mowing anything unless he was allowed to use the riding mower."

Tony, like others would realize, wasn't into "manual labor" and gave lawns that were to be mowed, a "lick and a promise". Which, literally meant that there were streaks of grass that were not mowed or to be more precise - it was a real slothful job.

The riding mower was Jesse's. Having seen Tony neglect the room he was living in, (dirty clothes thrown all over the place and it smelling like a men's locker room), the abuse he gave Jesse's truck that Tony used for the first 6 months he was out, the rudeness to me and the "macho male attitude that no woman is going to tell him what to do," I said "No." Tony started ranting, raving and slinging his arms around. He acted like a teenager being told he couldn't take the family car out on a Saturday night!

Charlie happened to be here that Saturday morning and he jumped all over Tony. Charlie called him "an insensitive jerk". Heated words were exchanged. I was crying. Jesse was upset, especially in light of the fact that Jesse hated confrontations of any kind. Jesse left the premises as not to be a witness to anything and not to be involved in anything. Tony shouted obscenities, vulgar obscenities to Charlie, then Tony stormed off to Mike's, stayed gone a few hours and pouted for three days without speaking to anyone.

Charlie told Tony "If I'd have known that you were going to be such a liar and con man I'd never have written a letter of support for you getting out, much less agree to your living here and being around us. We do not live like this. We work together and you are no longer welcome here." Charlie's blood pressure had risen to the point that he was beet red in the face. I had never heard him shout and get angry like this in over ten years of knowing him.

Charlie would later recall, "The only thing I specifically remember about jumping on Tony was the issue of edging the sidewalk down at 1885 Park. He would not work smart - get up and work while it was cool and work on it after a rain when the grass was tender and the dirt was soft. What he did do was shoddy!" Tony by this time was not making enough money to satisfy him and "it was boring" working the store. He applied for several jobs. However, he soon learned that being titled an "ex-con" wasn't winning him friends and influencing people. Prospective employers would not give him the time of day.

Mike Ator, with the Leather Factory in Missouri City suggested that he come and fill out an application for an assistant manager job that was going to be opening up. The job would have started out mid-$20,000, with benefits, and a chance of a promotion by having his own store.

Knowing that he didn't know the area of Houston too well, Charlie drove Tony the total of 260 miles round trip over there and back.

Charlie also paid the $10 going and coming for the toll road fees. Once again, Tony didn't pay for any of the expenses, nor, did he even offer, even with him having money in his pocket.

Reggie Johnson would later recall Tony telling him that "LinMarie had put an insurance policy on me and was trying to send me over there [to Houston] so that when I got killed she could collect the money."

I don't suppose Tony would ever realize, or if he did, he wouldn't want anyone that he was telling this lie to to know, that when a third party takes out a life insurance policy of any size on an adult, the person being insured would have to go through a physical and also sign for the third party to insure him or her. Tony never signed for any such policy, nor was there ever a policy of any kind taken out on him.

Through the Help Wanted section of the Beaumont Enterprise, Tony spotted an ad for a telemarketing company. He was able to land a job at Spherion, in Nederland, Texas, doing telephone marketing. Nederland is a small petrochemical community that rests about six miles south of Beaumont, just north of Port Arthur and within a 10 minute drive of where we lived.

If Tony could learn proper Spanish, he could get an added bonus. Thus, for the six weeks of his training, I worked with him every night on proper denunciations of Spanish or he used my Spanish training tapes (which he lost) to perfect his broken Spanish.

Each day, I cooked a full breakfast for him and sent him to work with hot meals or full course meals that all he had to do was warm up. Initially, because he didn't have any money - I gave him money for sodas, gas, and Jesse let him use his truck for six months.

After he started getting a check, and since he didn't have a checking account, Tony would endorse the check, I would get it cashed. In the evening upon his return, we would divide the bills out three ways and he would pay his part.

He would also be required to pay his way to go out to eat - which we frequently did when I was working my job as a Private Investigator and had not had time to cook. His mere $228 a week net did not go far, he would soon learn. But, what he told others was that I took his money and never gave him any.

He had never lived on his own, never had to pay bills like house notes, utilities, and he was very green and immature about those things. Moving on his own meant he would no longer be able to mooch off of people.

Before he moved to one of my rental properties, I sat down with him and helped him figure out a budget for his money. I showed him everything that he'd have to pay, helped him divide up when it was due, how much each week to put back for the due dates and suggested that he open himself a checking account, as well as a savings account.

I believe that he did both - though by the summer of 2004, he no longer had money in either account due to his purchasing of drugs, beer and other things [sex] for his girlfriend and other street girls. I call them "Gardeners" because they all go "ho-ing" at night.

It seemed that Tony was fascinated over having money - to the point of being obsessed about it. To him, money represented power. He went regularly to the plasma center to "give" blood. Even after his move to be closer to his job, he still sold his plasma. Reggie would tell him, "tell it like it is, you don't give blood you sell blood!" Tony told me, proudly, that he wanted to save some money. Money seemed to drive him. He wanted to be the first to be a millionaire.

Tony would tell Reggie, "Yea, I can hardly wait til I make my millions and I am in that long stretch limo headed to Austin, I'll call LinMarie and I'll show her…" Before it's all said and done, he may be in a long stretch white Blue Bird bus, heading north all right, but it'll be heading north back to Huntsville and the Texas Prison System!

After he stopped working at Two Hearts, I noticed invoices coming in. He had purchased a great deal of silver from another inmate at the Kennedy unit near San Antonio - which I would eventually have to pay for. He purchased supplies and tools for himself from a company in New Mexico to make silver items - which were put on my credit card - and, he'd "pay me back when he got his checks". That day never arrived.

My total debt for silver supplies and tools, thanks to Tony was more than $4,382. I take responsibility with the debt because I was stupid enough to trust Tony.

As the roles of our agreement were described, I was the only one who was supposed to purchase anything. Evidently my opinion and our agreement did not have any merit - Tony was "the man" and "no woman was going to tell him what to do - he'd had 18 years of people dictating to him what to do and no one was going to tell him anything especially not a woman."

Knowing that he would at some time cease to live with us, I had Tony start doing his own laundry at a Laundromat. He and Reggie agreed to meet and do their laundry. Reggie had to teach Tony how to use a washer, the right amount of soap to use, etc. I knew Tony wouldn't buy a washer/dryer and I knew he needed the experience of taking care of himself instead of me doing all the washing, cleaning, cooking and anything else that Tony construed as "women's work".

Later Reggie would tell me that Tony had told everyone that would listen that "LinMarie made me give her all of my check and never gave me any money" and, "I had $5,000 when I got out and she stole it all." Both statements could not have been farther from the truth.

Tony came with less than a $200 - in which $100 is the amount of money given to inmates upon their being released from prison.

Tony spent his first $100 on snacks, junk, satanic, horror, or science fiction movies that he wanted to bring to my house. I refused those latter three things to be brought into my home. And, when Tony would bring snacks - they were only for him - as he would eat them all rapidly or hide them in his room.

I wasn't raised around horror or satanic flicks, I didn't condone it with my own kids, and no one was going to infringe on me and my home in a manner I didn't approve of. Whether it was dope, prostitutes, satanic or Wicca stuff, cigarette smoking or heavy drinking - it wasn't happening at my house. I owned it. I had worked for it. I had refurbished it. And, no one, especially, not a person who daily was proving what a taker, liar, and user he was, was going to impose upon me.

Life got real strained in the house. Tony continued to go to Mike's. I could smell the scent of marijuana on his clothes when he'd come back. I never knew if he was partaking himself or just around those who were smoking it. I continued catching him making long distance calls to other parolees that he refused to pay for. Tony had also given the phone number to the store to a lot of guys before he got out. They would even try to call collect or want "the job he promised them."

What was really confusing me, was Tony's resistance to call his parents. In fact, at one point, Tony asked me to tell his mother do not call here, that when he was ready to talk to her, he'd call her.

And, he eventually did. He called and asked his mother to go get his birth certificate from Mercedes, Texas about 20 miles west of Harlingen. The truth of the matter was he could have gone eight blocks from my house to the Vital Statistics Bureau and gotten one himself - he just didn't want to spend $12.50 to get it - he'd rather someone else be inconvenienced and out the money.

Tony did make another call to his parents'; this time, to ask his Dad to give him money to buy a vehicle.

An old friend of mine who could purchase vehicles at auction found a 1980 something Bronco II. I told Tony that he probably needed to put new tires on it, fix it up, do a tune-up, change the oil, clean it out, fix a few things but basically he was buying someone else's problem.

I strongly urged him to purchase a new vehicle. He was opposed. So, Tony, Sr. sent Tony $3,000. Tony paid my friend $250 for finding the vehicle, getting the tags, etc. for him - but yet, later, Reggie would recall Tony saying "LinMarie stole that $250 from me by making me give her the money because she had helped me."

In fact, Charlie Ryan recalled that "when you suggested to Tony that he might be better off getting a new low cost automobile, I remember that I took him down to J-K Chevrolet in Nederland at the airport. I stayed in the Toyota while he looked at cars and talked to a salesman. It looks like he just humored you with his original intent of ignoring your suggestion. Considering the problems he later had with the Bronco, he should have heeded your advice."

Tony met with a sales representative and even took a test drive in a vehicle. Tony reported that his notes would only be $199 per month, as had been advertised. But Tony "didn't want the responsibility of notes." He'd "have my Dad just buy me something so I don't have to worry about paying him back."

I spoke to Tony's parole officer about the lies, deceit, and Tony not wanting to listen to reason about staying away from Mike's and wanting to watch the satanic videos. I told the parole officer that I was going to move Tony to 1620 Pennsylvania - sort of around the corner from where we were living - so that Tony would be on his own. I would rent him the house for $300 per month which was cheaper than any apartment that he would find. Tony had to get lights, water and phone turned on. And, not ever wanting to be without cable television, he got cable.

Jesse had found some furniture that a lady was throwing out that he had planned to put in a garage sale for $75.00. There was absolutely nothing wrong with the furniture and it was in immaculate condition. Tony agreed to give Jesse his $75. We also found a mattress on the side of the road that Tony could use that appeared to be clean.

My understanding is, after all this time, Tony is still using the mattress - but just recently, in 2004, threw out the couch and chair and bought something for $20. That means that he used the original couch and chair for over two years. We found other things in storage, like pots, pans, and I even gave him over $200 worth of towels that I had just purchased two days before he came home for the bathroom. I knew I would never use them or allow anyone else to use them because I knew Tony was already "getting blow jobs" from the "gardeners" over on Irving Street.

With approval from his parole officer, Tony was moved to one of my rent houses. He would live there for 6 months. I even worked him a payment plan, since I knew he didn't have any money to where he would pay me the rent for the first two months in installments - so that he could get on his feet. And, I did not even require a deposit as I normally do with others.

It would take a couple of weeks before being able to get Tony moved because someone else was living in the house and was about to move out - to be evicted was more the accurate word. Tony decided that he'd just sleep in his truck, but uses the bathroom, kitchen, and utilities in my house - that way "he didn't have to pay for anything." However, he did not move to his truck. But, he did continue to pay his fair share of the expenses he was incurring.

Jesse moved all of Tony's things over to the little one bedroom, one bath 480 sq. ft. house. It wasn't the Taj Mahal, but it was sure better than what he had grown up living in. It wasn't on the same line as the house he was exiting, but it was clean, there was plenty of air conditioning and heat. He could be on his own, and we had our privacy back.

There was one duffle bag semi opened and I noticed some dark colored woolen socks stuffed in there. I told Jesse to pull those out of there as I had not bought Tony any of those socks - all of his were white. Also in the hang up clothes were suits that belonged to Charlie Ryan that were 3 times too big for Tony.

When Jesse mentioned this to Tony, Tony responded, "Well, I might have some use for them." The fact was, Tony just wanted for the sake of wanting.

Reggie later stated, "Tony says you stole a recorder of some kind and his address books out of his bags." I believe that to be Tony manipulating in an attempt to get sympathy; it surely wasn't the truth.

But, for someone who came with nothing, it took Jesse 3 trucks full to haul Tony's things to 1620 Pennsylvania. All of his tools, silver items, clothes, everything was gone to his new home. There was no need for Tony to come back to my house. He was on his own.

That night, I slept better than I had slept since Tony's release.

I heard Tony had planned to go see *Delia, his old friend from the Rio Grande Valley. I phoned her and told her what all Tony had been doing, how he'd treated me and the rest of the people here, as well as his intrigue with sex, movies, drugs, drinking and partying.

She stated, "I am not surprised. I just felt in my soul that something wasn't all that he painted it out to be. I know my husband doesn't want him coming here and I will never give him a job or let him around my grandchildren."

*Delia told me that when Tony used to write her when he first went to prison that he would always put several Inmate Trust Fund forms inside her letters wanting her to send him money.

An Inmate Trust Fund form is what is used for people in "the world" to send an inmate money that goes into a trust account under his name and state identity number. Each time the inmate needs commissary or funds the money is transferred from his trust account.

I've since been to Delia's restaurant in the Rio Grande Valley. Without her realizing who I was, we chatted for a long time about her restaurant, the Rio Grande Valley, how it's a family owned business - and without a doubt, neither she nor her family should be subjected to the dark side of Tony.

Before the end of his six month lease was up, Tony moved out in the middle of the night. I was later told that Reggie helped him move. By this time, Tony had gotten sympathy from Reggie that I was so vile, money hungry and such a deceitful person that I couldn't be trusted. Tony had said "he felt like he was in a fish bowl" while living at the 1620 Pennsylvania address. Tony would tell Reggie when he moved out, "She [LinMarie] can keep that deposit I gave her." There never was a deposit.

When he lived at 1620 Pennsylvania, Tony was so paranoid that I was going to do something to him that he would put tape on the door jam of his vehicle to make sure that neither I, nor anyone else would get into it. One time, someone hung a dead rooster on the porch roof at the back door where he went in and out. The head was off and blood was dripping on to the step. Tony came running over to us - petrified - that someone was putting voodoo on him. Tony is a very superstitious person, but, typical of the voodoo and *curanderas* (Spanish for Witch Doctor) of the Rio Grande Valley and Mexico.

Tony moved to the other side of town into a trailer park that is considered to be 90% occupied by crack heads and prostitutes. The light brown colored trailer number five is at least a late 60's or early 70's model trailer. Very dilapidated. Very far and opposite to what he had lived in at my house or the little house at 1620 Pennsylvania. And, he was paying more in rent to this man, than he had to me. But, I would find it symbolic that he would revert back to the living conditions he experienced as a kid. Someone once told me that the fruit doesn't fall far from the tree.

I did call his new landlord, Mr. Meranda. I told him that he needed to watch Tony if he started using the torch down at the trailer when he was working on silver things. Tony almost caught my garage on fire once during his tenure at my house.

Perhaps that wasn't very nice. But, to explain why I did that is simple, in my mind. If anything were to happen to someone else's property, I would feel, in some manner, accountable because I was sure that Tony wasn't going to let anyone know that he had been in prison, much less that it was for arson, and surely not much less to report he killed a woman and their baby. In some weird way, I felt responsible because I was instrumental in getting him released.

I will admit that the first little bit without Reggie coming around bothered me. Reggie and I had been friends, at that time, for over fifteen years. When I needed furniture moved, I could call Reggie. I never "owed" Reggie. I would reciprocate with a hot meal on a Sunday afternoon or money - I knew he struggled on his salary and trying to raise two daughters on his own without support from their mother. Reggie was one of the first black men that I ever trusted.

And, despite, another lie from Tony that would later come out, Reggie was explicitly trusted here. Reggie would later tell me that "Tony said 'when we would go out of town she {LinMarie} would say don't tell Reggie anything because he would tell his girls and they would come over and rip us off.'"

I believe that was the beginning of Reggie realizing what a liar Tony was, since several times Reggie had been handed the keys to all of my properties and he had stayed in my property when we were out of town.

What I had told Tony was that "he needed to keep his mouth shut, don't tell people - no one - his business. He needed to stay to himself, date women who did not have children because I know how easy it is to get falsely accused of sexual assault, and stay away from swingers, drugs, and wild parties if he wanted to keep his feet on the ground." That is advice that I give to every parolee that I know or an inmate who may be coming out. To this day, I still say it is good advice.

Had Tony heeded at least some of the advice, his world may still be intact, his secrets still secrets and no one else hurt.

It just seemed that Tony was so adept to lying to people who were of lower mental status, stoned, or drunk that even he believed his own lies. Whereas, if anyone with any mental functions could figure out, nothing he said about me, Two Hearts, or our lives on the east side of Interstate 10 was true and could be validated as truth instead of the lies he was telling.

Initially, Reggie would call and report that Tony said this and that - mostly lies, nothing supportive or positive - that was for sure. I got real sick of hearing the lies about me coming from Tony and once again, I called his parole officer and asked that the parole officer instruct his parolee to keep me out of his problems and mouth.

Supposedly, several of Tony's parole officers told Tony to leave me alone. To hear Tony repeat it, though, parole thought it was amusing and that "Ms. Garsee is a real problem child."

Another yarn of Tony's was, "I left thousands of dollars of silver work in those showcases and never took any of it. I was so glad to get away from LinMarie." The silver items that were left in the showcases, were items that I had paid for and was still paying for even after Tony left Two Hearts.

On Wednesdays, we would go to Whataburger on College Street, across from the old Baptist Hospital that is now shut down for what, we call "our cheap date night". Whataburger, here in Beaumont, has a special on Wednesdays of "buy one get one free". We can both eat a burger, fries and have a drink for $6.26.

On one such Wednesday, Reggie, his daughter, her friend and Tony showed up. The first three spoke to us and were friendly. In fact, Reggie's daughter hugged my neck. Tony acted like a swelled up bullfrog. I found the relationship between Tony and Reggie to be amusing, considering a great deal of the letters I had received from Tony while he was incarcerated stated that he "never wanted to be around a f...... nigger again in my life."

I said, "Tony, don't you at least speak any more?" He scowled at me. Reggie would later say, "that ticked Tony off worse than if you'd have knocked him upside the head." After that, Tony went to the Whataburger on Dowlen Road.

His parole packet prologue continues to read, "Mr. Gonzalez is no longer hampered by the indiscretions and irrationalities of youth. He is now a mature man. He has grown not only in years, but emotionally, spiritually and academically. He is more than ready to go forth and accept the responsibilities which will be placed upon him. He will perform all that is required of him. He has been a model inmate and is ready and able to become a model parolee. He has come to terms with his incarceration and vows that he will never do anything which will cause him to be returned to prison if granted the privilege of parole."

When Reggie would call, I wouldn't talk to him. I didn't want to hear anything that was going on over there in their neighborhood. Tony's stay had caused me to have a heart attack and I was taking medication for hypertension. I didn't want to know anything.

I felt if I was oblivious to the wrongs Tony was doing, then I didn't have to deal with it in my mind. I already felt I had made a terrible, horrible mistake in helping him gain parole and regretted all of the financial and other help I had given him. I was almost to the point of being sick over it all.

In June, 2004, I received a real strange note in my newspaper box. It was a note typed on a half a sheet of yellow paper giving Tony's girlfriend's personal information. Her date of birth, her full name, social security number and drivers license number were all on this. And at the bottom typed was "J. Gonzales Tramp".

I phoned Reggie to ask him what this was all about. He said, "Well according to Eileena her boyfriend, Turner, said that he knew you and he was going to report Tony to you because Tony was doing drugs and whoring around with them girls."

I told Reggie that I didn't know Turner nor anyone named Turner.

About 3 weeks later, in the mail, I received another letter post marked in Beaumont on June 23, 2004.

It read:

> *"Mrs. Garsee*
> *I guess Mr. Parolee Jose G must be really stupid or feel he is untouchable. I heard through the grape vine that you had a score to settle with him.*
> *He is an arrogant M.F.*
> *I heard you was instrumental in getting him out early and the no good bastard didn't appreciate it. Well im going to give you some ammo to send him back.*
> *I'm no P.I. But I can find out what I want to know. Crack heads*

*love to talk.*

*Well Mr. Parolee committed a federal crime last year, in his quest to get rich he filed a fraudulent income tax return. Last year he paid this crack head name Deann 700.00 to let him carry her daughter Teresa on his income tax as his niece and I hear he got over 3000.00 back auto deposit in his bank. She tried to milk him for more money later for dope and he threatened to do to her if she didn't back off. That 11 y.o. girl never been to his trailer let alone lived with him 6 month as required by law I heard.*

*How stupid how stupid how stupid."*

There was no signature, nor any return address.

I phoned Reggie and asked him about this latest letter that I'd received. He laughed and said, "yea, and that girl, DeAnn wants to talk to you too."

I told him she could call me any time on my office number.

I went looking for this "Turner" guy over on Liberty Street where he supposedly had a wrecker service. I phoned the number listed on the sign on his gate. Turner answered the phone. I asked if we could meet. He agreed.

We met just a block down the street from his place at the Shell gasoline station at the corner of Martin Luther King and Liberty Street.

He stayed in his vehicle. I got out of mine and walked to the side of his truck. I asked had I ever met him. He stated "No." Then I explained what I had been told, what I had received and just from some of the statements he made, I believe this was the same person who wrote the notes to me.

The notes were typed by the same old typewriter. And, while standing there talking with him, I noticed something on his dashboard that was typed. The number "8" on the letters I had received made a funny mark and so did the "8"s on his paperwork in his truck.

I told Chuck Turner, that I did not want anything to do with Tony, didn't have any grudges against him, didn't want to send him back - as I figured Tony was messing up pretty bad on his own - and I didn't want any more message grams. I never received another one after that day.

I did later talk with Deann and she explained everything exactly as the mystery writer had said. I recorded the phone call, which I later gave to Tony's parole officer.

Tony had come to Deann asking to put her daughter, who has a Hispanic last name, on his income tax. Tony "had a strong desire to become rich. He even sells his blood every week to the blood plasma people and makes $180 a month doing that."

Deann would even tell "Tony is doing all sorts of things over there - from drugs, to drinking, to pimping and prostituting, you name it and he does it." A statement that Eileena and Reggie both would later confirm to me and others.

I would and will report any parolee who was or is not abiding by the law. The screw-ups that parolees have today have an immense effect on the outcome of future parolees. If a parolee acts out, then the ramifications affect everyone.

I gave a sworn to statement to the FBI, the parole office, and an investigator in the Jefferson County District Attorney's office. The parole office evidently confronted him about it. Tony was told to stay away from me and to rectify the wrong. I was warned by Tony's parole officer to be very cautious because she didn't know what Tony would do regarding me. The parole officer stated, "He's livid and unpredictable."

When Tony learned from his parole officer that I had brought in evidence against him, he thought he was going to be arrested and put back into prison. Wanting to have a "lasting memory" before he possibly would be locked away for years to come, Tony and four other friends had a wild week-end at a local motel, the Premier, on College Street, in Beaumont. According to sources that were in attendance, "there were enough drugs and booze and sex to last a life time."

Tony was told to "fix the problem". He went to the local IRS office, did an amended return, and has yet to pay any of the money back, to my knowledge.

Evidently, IRS' bite isn't as bad as they make people believe that it is. According to one of the street girls, "he thought he was going to go down for that one, so he sprung for a week-end at a hotel and everyone had an orgy and lots of drugs and booze. He wanted something to remember and dream about should he be sent back to prison."

Deann stated that she had gotten $700 initially from Tony for her letting him use her daughter on his taxes. Their agreement was that Tony would pay her half of what he got back. She later got $20 from him, possibly $10 more, and the last straw was when she was at the Scottish Inns and was about to be thrown out, she threatened Tony that she would call the 1-800 phone number to IRS. Only then, did Tony give her $50 more dollars to cover her room costs.

"He threatened to kill me like he did that girl. He said he knew how to kill people and burn them while they slept." Deann would recall during one of her "high moments". When an addict is on drugs, anything and everything comes out of their mouths.

I have been warned by several of the street girls to beware of Tony. And, people who are straight have also warned me to beware. "Tony's anger level is real high and everything that goes wrong is your fault."

Reggie once said, "Yea at one time he tried to get me to find some dirt on you so that he could use it against you. I told him, 'Tony you need to leave that alone.'"

Tony's strongest desire is to "outlive LinMarie so I can go piss on her grave." The humor, to me, in that statement is, I plan to be cremated. I figured as many women as Tony is reported to be having sex with, before too much longer he may not have a tool left to be able to use in any manner!

I don't recall what brought Reggie back around. I think that he may have gotten full of Tony's lies after 2-1/2 years.

On Sunday, October 31, 2004, he came over to go to breakfast with us. I'd been up late working a job and was exhausted but knew that I still had other work to do.

After eating, we all three decided to go to several flea markets. We spent the day together and it was like old times - enjoying the countryside, laughing and joking with each other. Little by little, Reggie started sharing things that Tony had said or done.

On November 2, 2004 Brenda Stancil, a reporter for *The Examiner Newspaper* called and asked if I could find a couple of crack addicts for her to interview. I didn't know where any of the old girls that had been around my area were. I phoned Reggie. Reggie made a few phone calls and immediately two volunteered.

One was Eileena, aka Cinderella. Eileena was "Tony's wife" according to the people in the trailer park where he lived. Her story came out in the weekly newspaper, *The Examiner.*

It reads: *"Cinderella, also a Beaumont prostitute and crack addict, responded similarly. "I know what I do is wrong but I have to do it." Cinderella has an 18-year-old daughter and the two women hang out at a man's house in a local trailer park. She works the streets at night selling her body to the highest bidder to buy the crack she craves. Her* boyfriend gives her some of the drugs she is addicted to, but not all that she needs. Neighbors say he is hitting on the daughter when Cinderella is out on the streets or simply out because of the drugs he gives to her. One neighbor described her as being completely lethargic at times and unable to communicate because of the drugs he supplies to her.

Cinderella herself told of a time last week when her man put a green pill or tablet in her drink that made it foam. As she drank it, she became dizzy and passed out. When she came to again it was apparent that the man who gave her the drink had raped her or had allowed others to do so. And, yet, she says she stays because she has nowhere else to go. She said, "It's funny. I love him and I hate him. I want to be with him and I want to be as far away from him as I can get."

Cinderella said the lowest point of her life came not long ago when she was sitting in a crack house smoking with a group of people she did not know well. "A black lady looked across the room at me and said 'I know you. You and your daughter came last Christmas with a church group to where I was staying and your daughter played the flute and all of you sang. It was so beautiful.'" Cinderella admitted with tears streaming down her fact that this was true. She had gotten her life straightened out and was off drugs. She and her daughter were in church and had agreed to use the talent they had to help the group during the holidays.

"And then, something bad happened, and I was back on drugs and here we are now. I'm working every night turning tricks to buy crack. I once was married and had a house and took care of my children. I know how to cook and I know how to clean. I can tell you that the road to becoming an addict starts with one hit of crack. You'll lose everything you've ever had and you'll do anything to keep the crack coming. Sell your body, break the law, steal, whatever it takes."

Prior to Brenda's interview with her, Cinderella and I sat in my van talking. "I'm so glad to finally get to meet you," she kept saying.

Then she asked the real question, "Will you tell me the truth about Tony because sometimes he scares me real bad - he has a dark side. I want to know the truth about why he went to prison."

I asked if she was sure she wanted to know. "Yes I have to know, my daughter is over there." she responded.

I told her what was on the incident report. A report that is public record, that even she could get if she went to Brownsville, Texas - it's all there - every police report, every confession that Tony gave, every statement from witnesses.

Evidently telling her that scared her fiercely. Later that night Reggie called me and asked what had I told that girl? I replied, "I told her the truth."

The next day, Reggie reported that Eileena had slept on Samantha's floor because she was too afraid to go back to Tony's. Eileena had some decisions to make and she needed to make them soon or possibly her or her daughter would end up like Lorinda, dead, somewhere in a burned out building.

I knew the looks Tony could give. I knew the fear that his facial jesters could make a weak person feel. I would not put anything past him. I figured that Eileena would get real tired of him, especially when she finally found out that Tony was pimping her daughter.

Sometimes mothers are the last to really know what is happening with their children. So, it was with Eileena and Laura.

Eileena is a pretty lady, and probably before her drugs and night life, she was even prettier. She is of medium height, slim, keeps her hair and make-up current and attractive. She is neat in appearance. She has, I believe, three children. The other(s) are married to well-to-do families and have nothing to do with her and Laura. Which leads me to believe, that at one time she was a good mother.

But, like so many other crack/pill addicted individuals, the dragon of desiring that first magnificent high that is received in smoking crack takes over. An addict will sell everything they have - even their souls and body - for that fix.

Reggie would tell it like this, "I jumped all over Tony for pimping out his stepdaughter, Laura. And, when that article came out in the newspaper, Sam and Lucky asked me if it were true that Tony was pimping out Laura. I told them, 'yes.'" "The other night he took Laura over to Pablo's house. Pablo's son had just come in from Mexico. Tony raised her blouse up and let the son massage her breasts. Then Tony told her [Laura] "take your pants off" and Laura did it and both of them screwed her. Afterwards Tony held his hand out for them to pay him."

Pablo told him, "Aye que juevos, Tony!" Translated into English, "My what balls you have Tony!" referring to him taking the money that girl had just earned.

"I told Tony that he was pimping her. And Tony said 'no I am taking from her $5.00 a trick towards her rent.' I said, 'that means you are pimping her.'" Reggie said.

On the 700 Club, Pat Robertson once stated that a man who was obsessed with Playboy and other such magazines had the mentality that a woman was an object only. She wasn't considered as God had created them, a help mate. The woman was an object - not respected, severely used and as later reported in Tony's case - abused.

Bettina would say "Tony was the only guy that I knew who could break up with a girl and still be friends. He had that trait as long as I could remember." However, knowing everything that is taking place in 2004, Bettina could not believe the dark side of Tony that she never knew. Perhaps the transition between girlfriends only prepped him for having innumerable mates and sex partners once he was released from prison.

Several of the "girls" have reported, "He's a kinky person for sure." One girl said that Tony got his "rocks off" by watching two girls have sex with each other then he would pile in on top of them and be having intercourse with one while doing something else to the other. One former cell mate from the Wynne Unit, in Huntsville, Texas wrote, "I have never heard from Tony since he left here. In all honesty while he was here his nickname was 'Porno King'. If you wanted pornography, just go find Tony because he had it even with it being contraband." My how I wish someone would have told me that before I assisted him in getting out.

One of the street girls said, "If you want to go to Tony's at night, there's a secret knock." I later found out that Tony wouldn't open the doors to his trailer if someone just knocked on the door - for fear that it would be the law and knowing that there were drugs inside his house.

November 2, Election Day. Reggie came by on his way to vote. We were talking politics, who we thought would win, when all of a sudden Reggie asked me if a parolee could vote. I said, "No, not until they are off of paper."

He said, "Well I read that article in the *Beaumont Enterprise* about parolees could vote after they were done with their time and did you know Tony has a voter's registration card?"

I asked him, "How did he do that?"

Reggie said, "I don't know but he does have one, because I seen it. On the blue side it shows his address over there on College and on the right side it has his post office box address on it."

I figured this was another prime example of how Tony was going to "beat the system" and do what he wanted to do. Neither Reggie, nor I, knows for sure if he voted or not. However, he must have lied on the application, when it asked if he had ever been convicted of a felony.

On Saturday November 6, I received a phone call from Eileena on my answering machine in the office. She said, " LinMarie this is Eileena King, the one that was dating Tony. He's pushed me down and hit me in the throat plus and he's pimping out my daughter. You'd think that he's invincible. I want to know what my options are to save my poor daughter. She's only 18. I'm moving to Vidor, my ex-husband's coming to pick me up. The telephone....I have to leave. I'll tell you as a mother I'm appalled how he can a testify to pimping this child out and tell her it's Okay. He's brainwashed her. Laura is slow but she's smart. She doesn't understand. She needs your help and I do too. I pray to God I will hear from you. Thank you. Good-bye."

I phoned a Sergeant with the juvenile division of the Beaumont Police Department and played him the tape. Since Laura is "slow" and has the mentality of a child, he was willing to visit with Eileena.

I couldn't find Eileena until Wednesday. She had other plans, but would "try to get in tomorrow to see him". I don't know if she ever did or not - and I sort of doubted that she would, considering that Tony was a source for her drugs.

I did find out that Tony is buying his drugs from a white girl and black man who live over off of Major Drive and College Street. Her name is "Sun Bunny". The black man's street name is "Mo". Everyone has a street name. Perhaps for multiple reasons - mainly no one knows who to say you are if they get caught by the cops and start spilling their guts or "singing like a canary" as it is called on the street.

I was also told that Tony was getting Zanaflex, a major prescriptive muscle relaxant from someone on his job for $3.00 per pill. In turn, he was giving them to Eileena to make her lethargic at times. That was the pill that she described to Brenda Stancil that caused her beer to foam up green. It was reported that on at least one occasion that Tony went to Mexico, he purchased muscle relaxants and had no apparent personal need (i.e. arthritis, pulled muscle, sprained muscle, etc.) for the medication. Even Reggie knew that Tony had bought drugs on two of their trips to Laredo.

The week of November 10, 2004, wasn't much better. Tony hadn't phoned Reggie all week-end because he had finally gotten a copy of *The Examiner* and read it. Tony was fuming. He even accused me of being the writer behind the story and using a ficticous name. Reggie said "No Tony, I met that reporter myself." Tony even accused Reggie of having brought Eileena over to my office. Reggie denied such a thing.

Tony did call to tell Reggie that the police had caught up with Monica and arrested her. Monica, another street girl, had broken into Tony's trailer some time back and stolen three checks. She took the checks to Super Cuts, got her hair done, bought some things, later took the things back and got cash. During the interview with Monica she implicated Eileen as an accessory to the crime. When the police asked Tony if he wanted to file charges against Eileen he stated "F... yes!" Reggie said, "I keep telling that stubborn little Mexican to leave it alone or it is all going to backfire on him. I keep telling him I am tired of holding his hand, wiping his nose and trying to keep him out of trouble, that he needed to let things die down and keep a low profile. No, instead he plans to run and call Ms. Parole Officer and wave her name around like it's some kind of magic wand! He is the most stubborn little Mexican I've ever met!"

On Thursday, November 11, Veterans Day, Reggie stopped by to pick up a jacket that I had bought for him and he was going to reimburse me for. I mentioned that I had to give Jesse a hair cut and imagined that I would need to give Ryan one this weekend. Reggie started laughing and said, "Yeah Tony said you used to charge him $10 every time you'd cut his hair." I just looked at him and shook my head. The myriad lies from Tony never cease to amaze me.

I think back and wonder why he hasn't gone home to see his folks. A round trip bus ticket is only $76 from Beaumont to Harlingen. Jesse has ridden the bus down to Harlingen to meet me there before and it was an easy trip. That's an extremely small price to pay to see parents that someone hasn't seen in well over 10 years now. Reggie even says that he has tried to encourage Tony to go see his folks.

I told Reggie, "His dad would croak if he knew what life style that boy was living up here. He'd never condone it for sure." Little did I know, at that time, that it wouldn't be long and Mr. Gonzalez, Sr. would be talking with me.

Tony's graduating class had their 20th Class Reunion in the summer of 2003. Tony was not invited to attend. Someone made the comment, "he'd better not show up." Perhaps Tony doesn't go home because he is quite sure of how people really feel about him and he may have to answer questions. It is more like he is *persona non grata*.

There is the old world custom among the Hispanics in South Texas and Mexico, similar to the Hatfields and McCoys - "an eye for an eye and a tooth for a tooth" mentality. Lorinda left siblings, friends and many family members. And, they are to this day, according to sources, "not settled with Tony yet".

A source, a street girl, stated that she confronted Tony about pimping out Laura. Tony's response was "Since when is it illegal to pimp anyone out? I am home having a beer and I have money in my pocket." Just having a beer is against his parole requirements.

Laura is an eighteen year old beautiful young lady. I find it amusing, ironic and even a little frightening that her name is so similar to the person that years earlier was killed by Tony. Lori was only eighteen and sexually active with Tony, the same age that Laura is now. According to all the street girls and Eileena, Laura's mother, Laura is slow and has the maturity of about a 14 or 15 year old girl. Tony buys her cigarettes, lets her smoke, buys her drugs, and even has a cell phone for her. Laura is at such an impressionable age that such thrills are important to a girl .

Laura is and Lori was cute. Laura is small in size, so was Lori. Laura has an outstanding, child like personality; Lori did, too. Laura is being snowed by Tony (that he's the only one who cares about her) and so was Lori (her belief that he could perform the abortion) with his intellect. One, has a living mother that loves her; the other, has a mother that loves the memory.

In the sex offender world, Tony's relationship with Laura is called "baiting" or "luring". The actions are protocols to gain a girl's trust, to convince the girl that the offender is the only person who loves her, who'll protect her - until the point that he has her totally convinced to do whatever that he asks her to... then it's "that's daddy's little girl." and she is rewarded with another hit of crack or a pack of cigarettes or maybe even a meal out.

These actions of luring, baiting and pimping out a young girl are perverted in the common person's world. It is not a standard practice of acceptance. And, I am quite sure, that Tony's family would not accept it either.

But, is he trying to replace the Lori he burned to death with this Laura? Is he trying to avenge Lori through Laura because of the years that he spent in prison? Is that the attraction? Or is he just trying to obtain monetary gains wherever, from whomever and however he can? What drives the obsession to be a millionaire?

I figured eventually Tony would measure Reggie by his own yardstick, and, it didn't take long before the irrational thinking of Tony's started happening. When the heat started coming around Tony, and his world began to unravel, Tony started pointing the finger at Reggie. Now it was Reggie's fault all of this was happening. It was Reggie's fault that he cheated on his taxes with the government.... It is always someone else's fault - never Tony's. Just like back in 1983, when his world was falling apart, Tony would call his friend, Juan Vargas whose brother was investigating Lori's death. Tony would try to do damage control by blaming everyone but himself.

I wondered if Laura is Tony's way of avenging the death of Lori - by making someone else who is so dramatically similar - who is eighteen years old, the same age Lori was at the time of her death and the number of years Tony spent in prison - suffer the way he did while incarcerated. No matter what his intent, this, too, in my opinion, is another life shattered by him.

Evidently destruction is going to follow or reach anyone who gets into Tony's way. On November 10, 2004, Tony supposedly filed charges on Eileena for being an accomplice to Monica, the lady who broke into Tony's place and stole some checks from him.

Damion, another of Eileena's boyfriends, supposedly sent a message to Tony, that Tony wouldn't have to worry about LinMarie putting him back into prison, Eileena was going to be the one to take him down. The woman that he really trusted will probably be the one to turn on him when she is brought to the police station.

About 11:00pm on November 14, Reggie phoned me. It seems that Mr. Gonzalez, Sr. had phoned him asking about Tony, Jr. Tony normally called every Sunday to tell them that he was fine, happy and everything was wonderful. Reggie told Mr. Gonzalez a father's worst nightmare or fear - everything negative and wrong that Tony, Junior has been doing and is doing - and I do mean everything.

Reggie left nothing out. Reggie even told him that I may have some things to add to the entire pot. Mr. Gonzalez stated that he wanted to hear from me too.

I phoned Tony, Sr. that night, without realizing it was after 11 pm. We talked for over an hour. Mr. Gonzalez sounded so disappointed, fearful for his son, embarrassed, and even expressed that he knew that Junior had a lot of enemies still living in Harlingen but that he didn't know any of these things that Reggie and me were telling him.

Mr. Gonzalez asked me three different times to send him copies of the article that was written in *The Examiner*. I assured him I would the first thing the following morning.

Mr. Gonzalez also stated that we, (me, Jesse & Reggie) were welcome at their house any time. Mr. Gonzalez scoffed at Junior's remark that Mr. Gonzalez was going to give him a vehicle, stating that this year (2004) that he and his other son had only worked less than 6 months all year due to people not hiring them.

I really felt sorry for Tony, Sr. and Catalina. Tony, Sr. suggested that he send Junior (the family's name for Tony) to Corpus Christi, Texas with Mr. Gonzalez' brother. I told him that Lori had family members in Corpus, or so I thought. He didn't know that.

He then suggested Dallas with another brother of his. I stated, "if there is a female child there 14 or above, I'd never subject any of my family members to Tony." He resolved that the only thing he could do was to put Tony's name in prayer - hoping for a miracle.

Mr. Gonzalez now knows about the drugs, the lies, the IRS, the pimping, everything. There was no stone unturned, including the lies about the $5000 that I supposedly stole from him and that I had an insurance policy on him. Mr. Gonzalez seemed to be really upset to learn that Tony turned down a $28,000/year job in Houston to stay among these whores. He was even embarrassed and displeased that Tony's name for me is "The Bitch". Mr. Gonzalez stated, "we do not condone that talk in my house." And, Tony probably knows that, thus, another reason for not going back to Harlingen.

I told Mr. Gonzalez that no matter what Tony does - everything is everyone else's problem - never his own. I also told him not to blame the girls, as Reggie has said, Tony's head is like concrete - hard and defiant. And, that Tony has burned all his bridges except for with people he can use or abuse.

I also drew the parallels for Tony, Sr. between Laura and Lori. That seemed to even increase Tony, Sr.'s concerns and interest. I went on to tell Mr. Gonzalez how Tony curses them. Tony has forever said, "my Dad blames me for my Sister's death"; "I do not know those people"; "I don't want nothing to do with them"; "they've never been there for me"; "my Dad would try to control me and I am a grown man"; "I've always hated them and will never go down there" - just on and on with derogatory remarks - just like Tony has with me. Perhaps his family and I have more in common than Tony would want to admit to.

The following morning, I spoke to Reggie before work. Reggie had full intentions of making sure that the parole office did know everything about Tony. The previous week Tony kept telling his parole officer, "I'm by myself" - Eileen and Laura were both caught over there that evening and all week-end for that matter. That was yet another lie of Tony to the parole office.. I photographed Eileena's vehicle at Tony's with a camera that dates and times it.

So many people have asked, "If Tony is doing all of this why hasn't he been revoked?" I have asked that question myself, but I know the answer.

A parole revocation will only take place when there is an arrest. To get reliable or credible parties to testify regarding a parolee's activities without an arrest, many times is insufficient for a revocation. A revocation is based on preponderance of the evidence and not reasonable doubt, as in a trial setting. There is much paper work that goes into a revocation - and they are costly. A parole officer wants to make certain he/she has a case - which is substantiated if there's an additional arrest - before he/she makes a move.

The Associated Press released an article, dated June 15, 2004, stating that the prison system within a year is going to be at an all time maximum overflow to the point of having to lease beds from private entities and counties. Thus, parole revocations are becoming less and less, in hopes that other arrangements can be made. Meaning, in my humble opinion that the common citizen has to cope with the Tonys of the world because there is no room at the Inn of Texas Department of Criminal Justice.

In Tony's case, there is more than "preponderance of evidence" - however, the parties involved will not come forward out of fear of Tony to file charges on him and some just are not credible. Some could attest to rape, battery, pimping, prostitution, having purchased and used drugs and alcohol with him, and I am sure many more charges.

November 15, 2004 out of curiosity I drove over to the west side of town where Tony was living. I stayed on the back street, Westwood, to where I wouldn't be noticed. Once again, I did find Eileena's truck there and I did take photos of her truck at his place. Even with Tony still proclaiming that Eileena is no where around him, with this photo he cannot say, "she is not staying here."

Reggie couldn't reach the parole officer, she was out sick. He did later in the week contact her and shared everything that he knew with her. The parole officer told him do not ever hesitate to call and report anything. Though, according to Tony, "parole people thinks anyone who calls up there and tells them stuff on me is just stupid and jealous and they (parole) do not take anything serious - especially if it comes from LinMarie."

I received another interesting phone call - "it seems that Trailer #14 at the Westwood Trailer Park is hot". Vernon is letting the girls pile up there and smoke crack, pot, or snort cocaine - whatever the drug of choice or availability is at the time and Tony is over there too." The call was anonymous, caller ID showed ID BLOCKED.

Over the week-end of November 20, 2004, Misty, a street girl, called me to report that Tony was wanting her to call the parole officer to tell her that I am paying her (Misty) to call and give invalid information to the parole officer to get Tony in trouble. Misty stated, "I told him that he was crazy I wasn't lying for no one - if he wasn't doing what was being said then why was he so nervous?" Damage control - Tony trying to do his best to do damage control.

This reminded me of Tony's phone calls to Juan Venegas prior to his arrest years earlier. He's nervous, but he wants someone else to cover for him. He wants to do damage control - make his story good, keep it straight, make it believable.

Misty, is such a sharp lady. She is articulate, smart, and shoots straight. If she doesn't like something - you will know it. She is a crack addicted prostitute. But, there is something about Misty that will keep you laughing - she has such an outgoing personality - a person that could be your friend for life - a person struggling with the dragon inside that demands crack from time to time.

November 22, 2004, I was in the west end of Beaumont working my Private Investigative job, looking for a girl that I had followed from Lumberton to one of the apartment complexes and couldn't remember which one. I had Jesse and Reggie with me, namely because it was dark, I didn't know for sure where I was going and it was raining cats and dogs.

Neither Jesse nor Reggie is investigators, but they go with me from time to time or when I feel nervous about a strange area. They stay in the van and are able to call 9-1-1 should I get into a bind or they think that I need police assistance or protection.

I entered the drive at Westridge Condominiums on Prutzman Street. I was going through the parking lot looking for Ms. Bennett's red car. As I rounded the corner near apartment 19, there stood Tony and another white man. When he looked at me, he paled as if he'd seen a ghost. I thought, "Oh brother."

We left, went directly across Phelan Drive, to the Shell station to get gasoline. Tony followed me there and stopped near my van and stared me down, as if to intimidate me. Reggie stated, "Well, Tony sure won't sleep tonight!"

Flukes happen. Who would've known that Tony was hiding out in the same place that I was trying to do my job? Why wasn't he at his trailer that parole believes he was living?

November 27, 2004, I received a call from one of the "girls". Tony was moving out in the middle of the night to the place on Prutzman that I had seen him at earlier in the week.

Eileena, was really put out with Tony because he had pretty much dumped her and now she was saying it was for a man! I have heard of divorces where the woman had left her husband for another woman, but never knew anyone personally that this had happened with. But, I figured the relationship between Eileena and Tony would mend itself when one wanted sex or the other wanted drugs.

Eileena did not look good at all. She appeared to have lost weight since the first time I had met her when Brenda Stancil had interviewed her for the article for *The Examiner*. Eileena was already thin then; now, she appeared to be frailer and more fragile.

With every story I am told regarding Tony, his present is equal to his past. He continues to belittle people to make himself look good, he continues to lie or fabricate stories to make himself appear to be the victim, he continues to try to do damage control when he thinks he's in trouble, he manipulates, he controls, he is deceptive, he is not a man of his word.

The latter was even true after he took his plea bargain of lesser charge of arson in the deaths of Lorinda Rocha and their unborn baby and he was incarcerated at the Wynne Unit in Huntsville, Texas where Tony began to try to appeal his plea bargain. It is an action that many inmates attempt to do once they are incarcerated, reality has set in, and they are sitting in a 6 foot by 9 foot cell with a cellmate that they do not even know, whose name is probably "Bubba". The two most common words inside prison are, "I'm innocent."

The hardest part of being incarcerated is not doing the time, but making the decision to make the changes that are necessary to become a better person and overcome the negative in your life. Then to follow through.

The first part of 2005, Tony moved closer to his job, somewhere in the Nederland/Port Neches area. According to the girls on the street, "things got too hot in Beaumont for him, but he and Eileena still comes over and buys their drugs over on Major Drive." Six months after his move, all data banks show he has not changed his address on his driver's license or motor vehicle registration.

It's been over seven months since Tony left Beaumont. I have noticed him making trips into my neighborhood, circling the block to try to see what is going on over at my house. He lives in Nederland. I live in Beaumont. His job is in Nederland. He has no reason, except for pure harassment, to circle my property. His actions are very obvious.

Even Reggie caught him passing my house in February, 2005, after following him down Franklin Street heading my way while Reggie was in someone else's vehicle.

Tony tells everyone, even today, that he should have never gone to prison. Evidently eighteen years is not near enough time for Tony

Gonzalez, Jr. to have any remorse for his own actions - much less have learned from his past mistakes. Justice for Lorinda and the other lives he continues to destroy will be when he goes back to prison for the rest of his natural life; or, there is a true repentance for his actions - whichever comes first.

Tony learned at a very young age to be a master manipulator. He perfected this while he was incarcerated and continues to manipulate circumstances, events and people to his best interest.

I would truly hope, if for no one other than himself and his parents, that Tony would become the man that I am sure his parents wish him to be. "To be who I am" does not always mean that it's the right path.

*"For every good tree bringeth forth good fruit; but a corrupt tree bringeth forth evil fruit. Wherefore by their fruits ye shall know them." Mathew 7:18, 20*

* Names have been changed for the protection of the persons involved.

*Note the Motel 6 where this took place at is no longer in existence. The Motel was replaced by a new Highway 77 and Highway 83 exchange.

Where Tony grew up at in Harlingen, Texas

Bowie Elementary - where Tony went to school

Coakley Junior High School - Tony & Bettina went to school together here

Harlingen High School - where Lori & Tony started dating each other.

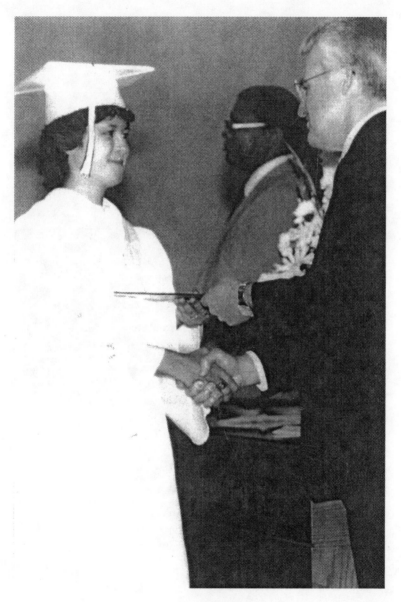

Lori Rocha at graduation

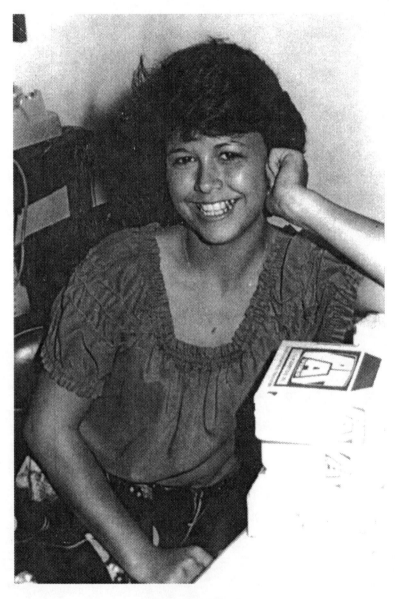

Lorinda "Lori" Rocha

Valley Baptist Hospital - Where Tony stole the chloroform

Inside of the Room 51 - Lori's jeans, keys and purse on the floor

Inside of the Room 51 - Lori's jewelry, make-up bag, cigarette case, pack of cigarettes - Tony had lit one, placed it in Lori's hand and waited for the sheets to engulf into flames.

Inside of the Room 51 - inside the bathroom - Soot covers everything

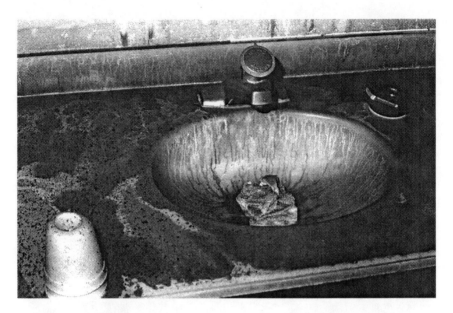

Inside of the Room 51 - a bloody rag inside the sink in the bathroom - severe smoke soot is everywhere

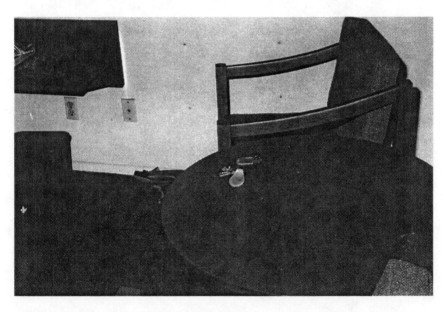

Inside of the Room 51 - the chair that Tony sat in smoking a marijuana joint while the smoke engulfed the room - Lori's shoes and keys in the photo as well

Room 51 at Motel 6 door open, Lori's car is in the middle and 3 officers from Harlingen, Texas police department stand guard

Inside of the Room 51 - Lori's shoes - where she left them before the sex, attempted abortion, fire and her demise

The entrance to Chamberlain Cemetery, Kingsville, Texas

Lorinda "Lori" Rocha's headstone in Kingsville, Texas

Wynne Unit or "Farm" (as the inmates call them) is part of the Texas Department of Criminal Justice (TDCJ)

Wynne Unit - in Huntsville, Texas is where Tony spent over 17 years for arson.

Tony being greeted at the bus station by LinMarie

Tony at his party on his first night home looking at the photos Bettina had put together for him

Tim & Bettina Elliott of Harlingen with Tony. Tony and Bettina used to be best friends.

Spherion hired Tony as a telemarketing person.

Taken at Tony's trailer on College Street - photo of Eileena's truck after Tony told parole that he was the only one there - and that Eileena wasn't with him

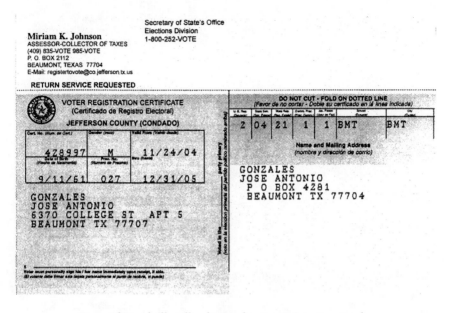

Copy of Tony's illegally obtained voter registration card

Photo of where Tony's orgy took place when he thought he was going back to prison

# Domestic Violence

Domestic violence is not a game. Domestic violence does not occur to only women and children. Domestic violence is not prejudiced - it occurs in all nationalities, all ages, all sexes.

The legal terminology of domestic violence, according to Law Encyclopedia is: "the continuing crime and problem of the physical beating of a wife, girlfriend, or children usually by the woman's male partner (although it can also be female violence against a male). It is now recognized as a antisocial mental illness. Sometimes a woman's dependence, low self esteem and a fear of leaving causes her to endure this conduct or fear to protect a child."

Domestic violence now includes verbal, physical, mental and emotional abuse. If you know someone or you are a victim of domestic violence, please contact your local police or sheriff's departments today. Seek help. Or for more information, you may contact one of the following organizations:

National Domestic Hotline - 1800-787-3224

www.domesticviolence.org

www.endabuse.org

www.WomensLaw.org

www.HelpForDomesticViolence.com

www.AbusedAdultResourceCenter.com

www.afccnet.org

www.wadv.org

www.dvmen.or

www.safe4all.org

# GET HELP TODAY

A portion of the net proceeds from the sales of this book will be donated to be used for educating the public, especially the youth, that domestic violence should never be tolerated and to report domestic violence. "Deliver me, O Lord, from the evil man; preserve me from the violent man…Keep me O Lord, from the hands of the wicked; preserve me from the violent man; who have purposed to overthrow my goings…."

Psalms 140: 1 & 4

Printed in the United States
58432LVS00006B/167